Investment Alchemy

*An Investors
Guide to Asset Allocation*

By
Guy E. Baker
Rick Jensen

Standel Publications
Newport Beach, California

Standel Publications

Standel trademarks include the following:
The Three Buckets of Investing
The Investor Matrix
The Compound Interest Story

This book was written to assist the reader's understanding of a very complex subject. In no way is this book meant to be a substitute for the professional advice and counsel of qualified experts who are trained to assist you in selecting the best investment portfolio for your situation.

First Edition, 1998

Investment Alchemy: 1998 ISBN 0-9647721-3-2
Standel Publications
Newport Beach, CA 92660

We invite you to send e-mail: guy@standel.com
or visit www.standel.com

Dedication

To our wives, Colleen and Nannette.
Thank you
for your patience,
love and continuing belief in our gifts

Acknowledgments

Anytime somebody sits down to write a book, there is pain. Pain for the author, the family, the production people and the editor. Investment Alchemy was no different. It was born from my need to communicate a simple, understandable approach to investing. The purpose was to de-mystify asset allocation and the stock market and to relieve some of the fear so many people have about something they can't control and barely understand.

I would like to thank my co-author Rick Jensen. His efforts to develop statistical evidence to demonstrate our principals was invaluable. Without his efforts, this book might never have been written. I also want to thank him for his patience and clarity as we discussed key concepts and how to present them in this book.

A major thank you to Ken Harris, our graphic artist. What seemed like a fairly straight forward job became a labor of love. His dedication, willingness to go the extra mile and the untold hours of devotion he spent making this book work cannot be described adequately. As you go through the book, imagine the amount of time it takes to make each graphic. What goes into designing each aspect of it, polishing it and fitting it into the text. Ken made this all happen. He took my scraps and notes and turned it into a work of art. Also to Connie, Ken's wife, for her willingness to input the many changes.

Obviously, a poorly written book is annoying. Suzanne Holly and Jill Boocock took my draft and made it readable. Without their efforts, this book would be full of who knows what type of errors. Jill's dedication and persistence, matching the edits with the final copy and polishing the galleys, brought together all of the pieces to its final form. Thank you, Jill.

I would like to also thank both my wife, Colleen and Rick's wife, Nanette. Their patience with this process allowed us to dedicate precious family time to its completion. If anyone achieves their retirement goals because of what they learned from this book, then you can thank these two wonderful women for their behind-the-scenes support.

I would also like to thank my son Todd for his leadership and follow through. He took the art and the copy and brought the book to completion. His willingness to work behind the scenes and receive only our thanks is a great witness to his servanthood.

And finally, I would like to praise our Lord for the gifts He has given all who worked on this book. Nothing happens by accident. It is only through His gracious mercy and love that anything can come into existence. He is the driving force behind the production of this book, from beginning to end, He proves He is the Alpha and the Omega once again.

Table of Contents

Alchemy (al'chem mee)
*The combining of independent elements to
create a more efficient whole*

Introduction

It seems like no matter what paper you pick up or magazine you read, there is an article about retirement. Retirement has become the great crisis in America. This book, **Investment Alchmey** was written to help readers become bolder with their investment strategy. And you know what? These pundits may be right. When I read about people who think they are going to retire in 15 or 20 years with $150,000 in savings, whoa! There is something desperately wrong here.

Here is a summary of America's greatest financial concerns as published in numerous magazine articles. Take the test and see how you do.

Can I retire comfortably at age ___	*Yes*	*No*
Will I have sufficient income when I retire?	*Yes*	*No*
Will I have to change my lifestyle when I retire?	*Yes*	*No*
Will I have enough income to pay my medical expenses?	*Yes*	*No*
Will my death or the death of my spouse affect our income?	*Yes*	*No*
Will I be able to financially assist my parents/family members?	*Yes*	*No*

Will I be able to help with the education
for my children/grandchildren?   **Yes**   **No**

These are important questions requiring thoughtful answers. Too often people brush them aside, figuring it will all work out. This is called denial and it is not a river in Egypt.

Have you ever thought seriously about what it takes to retire? It all depends on your standard of living, but let's do the math.

Suppose you are currently earning $50,000 a year and want to retire in 20 years. It would take nearly $1,000,000 to produce $50,000 annually if you could consistently earn 5%, year and year out, after tax. It's funny, but I have had people argue with me about this rate of return. They tell me it is too low. Yet, they have never consistently earned 5% net after tax on their money. Now, I grant you some might be able to do this or better, but most people are unwilling to take the risk needed to earn more.

As a benchmark, most pension managers set 6% as their targeted return. But it is better to be conservative than too aggressive—especially when it comes to retirement. Regardless, let's say you could earn 7%. Now it would take only $720,000 to earn $50,000 each year. If you could earn 12%, you would need less than $450,000 to do the same thing. Here's my point. Do you want your

You at work...

retirement to be based on your ability to earn 12% every year for the rest of your life or would you rather relax and know you can earn a little less and still meet

2

your income objectives?

Your retirement income should be totally dependent upon your ability to create a consistent income from your capital. There are basi-

...your money at work!

cally, only two ways for you to earn an income: you can work or your money can work. I discussed these two concepts thoroughly in my first book, **Baker's Dozen**. It seems like everyone would agree your goal is to have enough money working at retirement. Ask yourself this question: when you retire, don't you want to have enough money to produce an income for the balance of your life? I would think so.

THE BIG QUESTION

Okay, so how much income will you need to meet your objectives? One way to approach this is to answer a different question. Do you want to live off the capital you have or just the interest it earns? Why is this important?

If you live off the interest, then your capital will always be there and you never have to worry about running out of time or money. Your capital will continue producing income through the power of compound interest. But if you elect to live off the capital, then time is working against you. Your capital slowly reduces and eventually you run out of capital and interest. Look at Chart 1. If you had $700,000 paying you $50,000 per year, you'd be broke in 25 years if you systematically liquidated your capital.

It should come as no surprise that people are living

3

$50,000 income / 5% Net Rate of Return (Chart 1)					
Spending Capital			Preserving Capital		
Year	Assets	Income	Year	Assets	Income
	700,000.00			1,000,000.00	
1	685,000.00	50,000.00	1	1,000,000.00	50,000.00
2	669,250.00	50,000.00	2	1,000,000.00	50,000.00
3	652,712.50	50,000.00	3	1,000,000.00	50,000.00
4	635,348.13	50,000.00	4	1,000,000.00	50,000.00
5	617,115.53	50,000.00	5	1,000,000.00	50,000.00
6	597,971.31	50,000.00	6	1,000,000.00	50,000.00
7	577,869.87	50,000.00	7	1,000,000.00	50,000.00
8	556,763.37	50,000.00	8	1,000,000.00	50,000.00
9	534,601.54	50,000.00	9	1,000,000.00	50,000.00
10	511,331.61	50,000.00	10	1,000,000.00	50,000.00
11	486,898.19	50,000.00	11	1,000,000.00	50,000.00
12	461,243.10	50,000.00	12	1,000,000.00	50,000.00
13	434,305.26	50,000.00	13	1,000,000.00	50,000.00
14	406,020.52	50,000.00	14	1,000,000.00	50,000.00
15	376,321.55	50,000.00	15	1,000,000.00	50,000.00
16	345,137.62	50,000.00	16	1,000,000.00	50,000.00
17	312,394.50	50,000.00	17	1,000,000.00	50,000.00
18	278,014.23	50,000.00	18	1,000,000.00	50,000.00
19	241,914.94	50,000.00	19	1,000,000.00	50,000.00
20	204,010.69	50,000.00	20	1,000,000.00	50,000.00
21	164,211.22	50,000.00	21	1,000,000.00	50,000.00
22	122,421.78	50,000.00	22	1,000,000.00	50,000.00
23	78,542.87	50,000.00	23	1,000,000.00	50,000.00
24	32,470.02	50,000.00	24	1,000,000.00	50,000.00
25	-15,906.48	50,000.00	25	1,000,000.00	50,000.00

longer today than ever. To provide absolute security, you need an income you **cannot** outlive. This requires significantly more capital than most people think.Why?

Look at Chart 2 and Chart 3. Notice the annual income is $50,000. But if you factor in the loss of purchasing power caused by inflation—look what happens. After only 10 years (Chart 2) your $50,000 is worth only $28,099. Even if inflation is 3.7%, the loss in purchasing power is $15,705 (Chart 3). We've all read a lot about inflation, but exactly what is inflation? I think of it this way.

> *If you are not earning an income and you are spending everything your capital is earning, then how can your money grow?*

Suppose you went to the grocery store and bought a basket of food and other products. Today, filling your shopping cart might cost you $100. But in five years, that same exact basket might cost $125 because the prices have gone up. In 10 years, our mythical basket might now cost $175. Inflation is the economic term which describes the increase in prices. Whether it is food, rent, gasoline, haircuts, or whatever, rising prices cause a reduction in the amount of goods and services you can acquire at a given time for a specified amount of money. Likewise, falling prices (deflation) cause the amount of goods and services you can purchase to increase for the same amount of money.

Economists are constantly trying to measure the rate of increase and decrease in consumer prices. They try to figure out how fast the prices are rising over time. If $100 increases to $106 and then to $113, the rate of increase is 6%. That is a devastating increase in prices

Average Inflation rate for past 25 years = 5.6% (Chart 2)				
Year	Assets	Income	Inflation Adjusted	Loss of purchasing power
1	1,000,000.00	50,000.00	47,200.00	2,800.00
2	1,000,000.00	50,000.00	44,556.80	5,443.20
3	1,000,000.00	50,000.00	42,061.62	7,938.38
4	1,000,000.00	50,000.00	39,706.17	10,293.83
5	1,000,000.00	50,000.00	37,482.62	12,517.38
6	1,000,000.00	50,000.00	35,383.60	14,616.40
7	1,000,000.00	50,000.00	33,402.11	16,597.89
8	1,000,000.00	50,000.00	31,531.60	18,468.40
9	1,000,000.00	50,000.00	29,765.83	20,234.17
10	1,000,000.00	50,000.00	28,098.94	21,901.06
11	1,000,000.00	50,000.00	26,525.40	23,474.60
12	1,000,000.00	50,000.00	25,039.98	24,960.02
13	1,000,000.00	50,000.00	23,637.74	26,362.26
14	1,000,000.00	50,000.00	22,314.03	27,685.97
15	1,000,000.00	50,000.00	21,064.44	28,935.56
16	1,000,000.00	50,000.00	19,884.83	30,115.17
17	1,000,000.00	50,000.00	18,771.28	31,228.72
18	1,000,000.00	50,000.00	17,720.09	32,279.91
19	1,000,000.00	50,000.00	16,727.76	33,272.24
20	1,000,000.00	50,000.00	15,791.01	34,208.99
21	1,000,000.00	50,000.00	14,906.71	35,093.29
22	1,000,000.00	50,000.00	14,071.94	35,928.06
23	1,000,000.00	50,000.00	13,283.91	36,716.09
24	1,000,000.00	50,000.00	12,540.01	37,459.99
25	1,000,000.00	50,000.00	11,837.77	38,162.23

Introduction

Year	Assets	Income	Inflation Adjusted	Loss of purchasing power
1	1,000,000.00	50,000.00	48,150.00	1,850.00
2	1,000,000.00	50,000.00	46,368.45	3,631.55
3	1,000,000.00	50,000.00	44,652.82	5,347.18
4	1,000,000.00	50,000.00	43,000.66	6,999.34
5	1,000,000.00	50,000.00	41,409.64	8,590.36
6	1,000,000.00	50,000.00	39,877.48	10,122.52
7	1,000,000.00	50,000.00	38,402.02	11,597.98
8	1,000,000.00	50,000.00	36,981.14	13,018.86
9	1,000,000.00	50,000.00	35,612.84	14,387.16
10	1,000,000.00	50,000.00	34,295.16	15,704.84
11	1,000,000.00	50,000.00	33,026.24	16,973.76
12	1,000,000.00	50,000.00	31,804.27	18,195.73
13	1,000,000.00	50,000.00	30,627.51	19,372.49
14	1,000,000.00	50,000.00	29,494.30	20,505.70
15	1,000,000.00	50,000.00	28,403.01	21,596.99
16	1,000,000.00	50,000.00	27,352.10	22,647.90
17	1,000,000.00	50,000.00	26,340.07	23,659.93
18	1,000,000.00	50,000.00	25,365.49	24,634.51
19	1,000,000.00	50,000.00	24,426.96	25,573.04
20	1,000,000.00	50,000.00	23,523.16	26,476.84
21	1,000,000.00	50,000.00	22,652.81	27,347.19
22	1,000,000.00	50,000.00	21,814.65	28,185.35
23	1,000,000.00	50,000.00	21,007.51	28,992.49
24	1,000,000.00	50,000.00	20,230.23	29,769.77
25	1,000,000.00	50,000.00	19,481.71	30,518.29

over time. Remember, money doubles every 12 years at 6% (See Rule of 72). If the prices rise slower, the rate might be only be 2%. Either way, it's this rate of increase that we call inflation.

Inflation is measured as a percentage of a base price established in a specified year. For instance, the prices may be measured in 1968 dollars (i.e. what a basket of goods would cost in 1968.) As the price level rises, you are able to purchase fewer goods and services for the same income.

Inflation is not an obvious problem while you are working and accumulating capital. For someone who is working, inflation is often offset by steady increases in income and additional savings. It masks the increasing prices. Presumably, you will get a raise, earn more income or your investments may compound faster. But when you retire, you will have a problem keeping up. If you are not earning an income and you are spending everything your capital is earning, then how can your money grow?

Remember the original $50,000 retirement model? I asked how much capital would be required to create a

---

The Chain of Compound Interest
"Rule of 72"

To find the length of time required to double money, divide 72 by the interest rate.

$$10\%\overline{)\,72}\;\;=\;7.2\text{ Years} \qquad 7.2\%\overline{)\,72}\;\;=\;10\text{ Years}$$

To find the interest rate when money doubles, divide 72 by the years involved.

$$8\text{ Years}\overline{)\,72}\;\;=\;9\% \qquad 12\text{ Years}\overline{)\,72}\;\;=\;6\%$$

WHAT will my $50,000 income be worth at age 65?

- It will purchase only $38,121 worth of goods and services at age 65.
- This chart shows income target and the effect of inflation on your purchasing power.

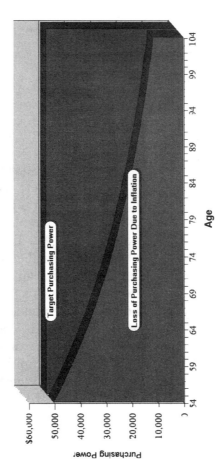

Assumptions:
  3% inflation rate
  $50,000 desired purchasing power at retirement

If you are 54 today and want $50,000 income at age 65, look at what happens. Your target income has declined to $38,121 at age 65. It will further decline if you do not take action.

9

level income of $50,000 annually. The answer was $1,000,000. If we factor in inflation, the answer is a lot different. A $50,000 income in 20 years might only purchase $23,000 worth of goods and services in today's dollars (see Chart 2, again). If you want to purchase a constant $50,000 of goods and services, you will need to protect your real purchasing power. Suppose the real purchasing power produced by your capital has dropped to $23,000. You will either need your capital to produce more income or you will have to supplement your income. The third alternative is virtually unthinkable— you will have to spend some of your capital.

Let's be sure we clearly understand this problem because this issue is at the heart of the retirement crisis we all face. Suppose you had $1,000,000 in your retirement account and it was, in fact, earning, $50,000 annually. Most people would say there's no problem. But suppose this is 20 years later and $50,000 is purchasing only $23,000 of goods and services. Remember, you still have $50,000 of income every year. This did not change and you still have $1,000,000 of original capital. But as you look in your shopping basket, you can see you have considerably less than you had 20 years ago.

You survey your alternatives and ponder your three choices. You can live with fewer goods and services. You can supplement your income with other income. Or, you could start spending your capital. In other words, you could decide to use some of your $1,000,000 of capital to maintain your standard of living. Look at Chart 2 and see what a dramatic impact inflation can have on your purchasing power. Notice that in ten years, you will have $15,704 (Nearly 30%) less purchasing power.

Please understand, I am not trying to tell anyone

what to do nor am I trying to scare anyone. Rather, I want to point out how inflation is the hidden problem. It is hidden from those who have not thoroughly measured this risk. Most people think the risk of losing their capital is their only risk.

But inflation is a much more insidious risk!

Fortunately, there is another solution. You could invest your $1,000,000 in an investment which will start earning more than the 5% you are now getting. "Oh no" you say. "I can't take the risk of losing my money. My brother-in-law invested in a stock that collapsed

The Baker's Dozen	
1.	Establish a Consistent Savings Plan
2.	Control What You Spend
3.	Only Use Debt for Leverage
4.	Set Lifetime Goals and Investment Objectives
5.	Make Your House a Profitable Investment
6.	Guarantee Your Family's Security
7.	Don't Be Greedy
8.	Invest Wisely and Don't Spend the Money Money Makes
9.	Study How Others Have Made Money
10.	Invest in Who You Know and What You Know
11.	Invest Regularly and Diversify Your Risk
12.	Constantly Review Your Progress and Your Goals
13.	Wealth is a State of Mind

and he lost *all* of his money. I could not afford to lose everything. I would rather live with $23,000 of purchasing power than risk losing my capital. I'll just have to cut my spending."

You are right. No one can afford to lose his capital. That's Rule #8 in **Baker's Dozen**. There is definitely more risk when you invest in assets which might earn more than just a secure rate of interest. However, you must remember, there are the two risks you actually face—the inflation risk and the potential loss of capital. Historically, inflation has averaged 5.6% for the last 25 years, while the U.S. stock market has grown at a rate of nearly 12%. Certainly, there have been some down cy-

If the Average Inflation rate for past 25 years was 5.6% (Chart 4)

Year	Assets	Income	Inflation Adjusted	Loss of purchasing power	Necessary Dollars To make up	Remaining Assets	Adjusted Purchasing Power
1	1,000,000.00	50,000.00	47,200.00	2,800.00	2,800.00	997,200.00	50,000.00
2	997,200.00	49,860.00	44,432.04	5,567.96	5,879.76	991,320.24	50,000.00
3	991,320.24	49,566.01	41,696.53	8,303.47	9,259.49	982,060.74	50,000.00
4	982,060.74	49,103.04	38,993.87	11,006.13	12,960.64	969,100.10	50,000.00
5	969,100.10	48,455.01	36,324.41	13,675.59	17,005.98	952,094.12	50,000.00
6	952,094.12	47,604.71	33,688.51	16,311.49	21,419.69	930,674.44	50,000.00
7	930,674.44	46,533.72	31,086.49	18,913.51	26,227.42	904,447.02	50,000.00
8	904,447.02	45,222.35	28,518.66	21,481.34	31,456.39	872,990.63	50,000.00
9	872,990.63	43,649.53	25,985.29	24,014.71	37,135.45	835,855.18	50,000.00
10	835,855.18	41,792.76	23,486.65	26,513.35	43,295.22	792,559.96	50,000.00
11	792,559.96	39,628.00	21,022.97	28,977.03	49,968.12	742,591.83	50,000.00
12	742,591.83	37,129.59	18,594.48	31,405.52	57,188.55	685,403.29	50,000.00
13	685,403.29	34,270.16	16,201.38	33,798.62	64,992.90	620,410.39	50,000.00
14	620,410.39	31,020.52	13,843.85	36,156.15	73,419.78	546,990.61	50,000.00
15	546,990.61	27,349.53	11,522.05	38,477.95	82,510.03	464,480.57	50,000.00
16	464,480.57	23,224.03	9,236.12	40,763.88	92,306.93	372,173.64	50,000.00
17	372,173.64	18,608.68	6,986.18	43,013.82	102,856.26	269,317.38	50,000.00
18	269,317.38	13,465.87	4,772.33	45,227.67	114,206.51	155,110.87	50,000.00
19	155,110.87	7,755.54	2,594.66	47,405.34	126,408.95	28,701.93	50,000.00
20	28,701.93	1,435.10	453.23	49,546.77	139,517.85	-110,815.92	50,000.00
21	-110,815.92	-5,540.80	-1,651.90	51,651.90	153,590.61	-264,406.54	50,000.00
22	-264,406.54	-13,220.33	-3,720.71	53,720.71	168,687.94	-433,094.48	50,000.00
23	-433,094.48	-21,654.72	-5,753.19	55,753.19	184,874.03	-617,968.51	50,000.00
24	-617,968.51	-30,898.43	-7,749.33	57,749.33	202,216.73	-820,185.23	50,000.00
25	-820,185.23	-41,009.26	-9,709.16	59,709.16	220,787.77	-1,040,973.01	50,000.00

Charts 4 and 5 shows what happens if you elect to spend down your capital. At 5.6% inflation you are out of capital in the 20th year. If inflation is 3.7% your capital is gone in the 24th year.

If the Average Inflation rate for past 25 years was 3.7% (Chart 5)

Year	Assets	Income	Inflation Adjusted	Loss of purchasing power	Necessary Dollars To make up	Remaining Assets	Adjusted Purchasing Power
1	1,000,000.00	50,000.00	48,150.00	1,850.00	1,850.00	998,150.00	50,000.00
2	998,150.00	49,907.50	46,282.67	3,717.33	3,854.87	994,295.13	50,000.00
3	994,295.13	49,714.76	44,398.08	5,601.92	6,024.13	988,270.99	50,000.00
4	988,270.99	49,413.55	42,496.31	7,503.69	8,367.80	979,903.20	50,000.00
5	979,903.20	48,995.16	40,577.44	9,422.56	10,896.43	969,006.77	50,000.00
6	969,006.77	48,450.34	38,641.55	11,358.45	13,621.12	955,385.65	50,000.00
7	955,385.65	47,769.28	36,688.73	13,311.27	16,553.58	938,832.07	50,000.00
8	938,832.07	46,941.60	34,719.08	15,280.92	19,706.10	919,125.97	50,000.00
9	919,125.97	45,956.30	32,732.68	17,267.32	23,091.65	896,034.32	50,000.00
10	896,034.32	44,801.72	30,729.64	19,270.36	26,723.82	869,310.50	50,000.00
11	869,310.50	43,465.52	28,710.06	21,289.94	30,616.96	838,693.54	50,000.00
12	838,693.54	41,934.68	26,674.04	23,325.96	34,786.11	803,907.43	50,000.00
13	803,907.43	40,195.37	24,621.69	25,378.31	39,247.13	764,660.30	50,000.00
14	764,660.30	38,233.02	22,553.12	27,446.88	44,016.64	720,643.67	50,000.00
15	720,643.67	36,032.18	20,468.45	29,531.55	49,112.14	671,531.52	50,000.00
16	671,531.52	33,576.58	18,367.79	31,632.21	54,552.02	616,979.50	50,000.00
17	616,979.50	30,848.98	16,251.28	33,748.72	60,355.57	556,623.93	50,000.00
18	556,623.93	27,831.20	14,119.04	35,880.96	66,543.09	490,080.84	50,000.00
19	490,080.84	24,504.04	11,971.19	38,028.81	73,135.86	416,944.98	50,000.00
20	416,944.98	20,847.25	9,807.87	40,192.13	80,156.26	336,788.72	50,000.00
21	336,788.72	16,839.44	7,629.21	42,370.79	87,627.76	249,160.96	50,000.00
22	249,160.96	12,458.05	5,435.36	44,564.64	95,575.00	153,585.97	50,000.00
23	153,585.97	7,679.30	3,226.46	46,773.54	104,023.84	49,562.12	50,000.00
24	49,562.12	2,478.11	1,002.65	48,997.35	113,001.44	-63,439.31	50,000.00
25	-63,439.31	-3,171.97	-1,235.91	51,235.91	122,536.25	-185,975.56	50,000.00

cles during that period. But which risk is guaranteed to happen? Inflation or loss of capital? And which risk is more likely to impact you?

Inflation will always be a fact of life. You cannot have a growing economy without rising price levels. The goods and services you can purchase must always cost more, otherwise, there will be no growth.

I decided to write **Investment Alchemy**, in order to help others understand how to protect themselves against inflation and loss of capital. With the assistance of my partner, Rick Jensen, we have set out to explain what we feel are the issues an investor needs to consider. I wish I could tell you we had all of the answers. We certainly don't! In fact, just to prove it, let me give you a little bit of my own investment history.

I entered the financial services industry in 1966. I immediately decided I would become licensed to sell mutual funds. With only a handful of exceptions in 30 years, I never sold any equity products to my clients. In fact, I purposely chose to avoid this aspect of the financial services industry. Now don't misunderstand me. I stayed current. I followed the markets. I read the myriad of magazines we call financial "pornography," which is designed to titillate and motivate readers to purchase their information. In general, there is little value in the information or analysis they provide. I lusted after the financial fortunes which were made in the stock market on selected issues. But I could not figure out how to invest consistently for myself or my clients. I was not aware of any investment system which would work over the long run—a system that made sense to me. So I stayed on the sidelines and watched.

If you know what happened during those intervening years, then you know fortunes were made and fortunes were lost. But the statistics remained the same. The U.S. domestic market continued to grow at 10%–12%. Yet, I missed all of it. In fact, more than 95% of all Americans have missed it. Most Americans will probably reach retirement without enough capital to retire. They will be dependent upon family or government programs to sustain their lifestyles. Obviously, there is no guaranteed system out there for these people or it would be shouted from the roof tops. Somebody would be using it and telling everyone else. Do you really think something this important could be kept a secret?

I had a dilemma. Market research tells us these consumers want their product provider to be honest and fair. Let's face it, wouldn't you want your trusted advisor to offer you top quality products? Well, that's exactly what I have always wanted to do. But I always felt the costs were too high for the consumer. More importantly, my crystal ball was too cloudy to tell me what I should offer. When the proverbial monkey could randomly pick a better portfolio than most professionals, I knew I didn't have a chance. Recent studies have determined 85% of the professional portfolio managers underperform the market. In other words, if you just bought a broad cross section of the U.S. stock market and held on to it, you would do better than most of the professional money managers. A mutual fund which buys every stock in a specific segment of the market is called an index fund. It is based on the performance of a broad cross-section of the stock market.

> *Most Americans will reach retirement without enough capital to retire.*

I discovered that many of my clients had lost significant sums of money chasing various investment schemes. Certainly, some of them did okay for a time, but in the long run, the stock market out-performed them. Maybe you have even suffered from some of these "recommendations" being sold in the '70s and '80s.

The bottom line was simple. As a professional I needed to understand how to do this for myself. I was not going to make my career based on selling products, which I did not understand, to my trusted clients. As a result, I concentrated on selling conservative, low yield products—like life insurance.

> *There is now significant research available which shows how to manage the randomness of the market.*

SO WHAT CHANGED?

You may wonder why I am now writing a book about investing and attempting to help you navigate these treacherous waters. I have asked myself this very question. Here are the answers I believe have motivated me to write this book.

Advisors are stewards of their clients' welfare and assets. I believe I have a professional obligation to either help clients or introduce them to a professional who can help. I am tired of watching people lose money because they don't know where to go or what to buy. I cannot eliminate the financial risks, but I can certainly eliminate the integrity risks.

As I observed the recommendations and actual performance of other investment advisors over the last 30 years, it became obvious I could do as well as, if not better, than most of them. This may sound arrogant, but many investment advisors have failed to really consider their clients' welfare.

Retirement is a huge issue for most people. I feel a compelling obligation to help my clients with this problem. I also feel I am qualified to bring reason to this situation with my 30 years of experience.

There is now, significant research available which shows how to manage the randomness of the market. Rick and I both know we can't make anybody rich, but I think we can help clients build a strategy which will protect their "core" dollars—the dollars you can't ever afford to lose. I also think our ideas can augment your retirement income and help protect your capital and income from inflation. That's what this book is really about. It's about how you can accomplish sustained growth and protect your core dollars from inflation.

We believe this service is best provided for a fee rather than a commission—a lower fee than we see currently being charged by many advisors. Why? Frankly, we believe the market is overcharging the consumer for these services. Through technology, there are now very cost-efficient, competitive computer systems available to manage money for 50% or less than what most advisors are charging.

The purpose of this book is to explain what I have learned about investing these "core" dollars. The dollars you do not want to risk but are especially subject to the ravages of inflation. I do not want anyone to speculate with these dollars. I am not interested in building a portfolio which is *expected* to earn 20%-25% annually, year in and year out. This book is only about managing the money you are not willing to lose.

Investment Alchemy is about a process which will protect you. I want you to understand the rudiments of

Modern Portfolio Theory (MPT). This concept was awarded the Nobel Prize for economics in 1990. Hundreds of pension plans use MPT principles to manage their funds. If you like the concept, then you may very well want to find someone who can make it work for you. Remember, there are two risks and one absolutely guarantees the loss of purchasing power (inflation). The other risk is subject to the movement of the market and historically has offset the loss caused by inflation. If you don't like our system for combating this fundamental problem, then I invite you to show me a system you think will consistently work better. I am always open to better ideas.

Here is a list of critical issues I think an investor should understand as he/she evaluates other systems for investing his/her "core" dollars:

1. No sales loads (Front or Back End loads)
2. Low cost advisory fees (less than 1.0% annually)
3. Low cost for investing the funds (less than 50 basis points)
4. Low trading costs
5. Low expense ratios
6. Protection against excessive taxation of profits
7. A measurable benchmark for performance
8. Wide diversification of your assets
9. Immediate access to your money

Rick and I have searched the market, high and low for the very best method to achieve these objectives. Modern Portfolio Theory—using the asset mix described in this book, is the only method we know of which can consistently meet most of these objectives.

1
The Money Machine

Imentioned there are only two ways to earn money. There is man at work and there is money at work. I say "man" here, because in the ancient Hebrew, the word for man (adam) distinguishes between mankind as a grouping of people vs. a man (kakar) when it was used to describe the male of the species. So when you read "he" or "man" in this book, please accept that I mean adam. All of us are individuals, unique and distinct and I am not trying to differentiate between male and female.

When we first start working, all we have is "man at work." Unless, of course, you belong to the lucky "gene" club. If you inherited wealth, then your money issues are different. But for most of us, the only thing we inherited was the opportunity to earn a living.

FOURS WAYS WE SPEND MONEY

As we earn a living, the money we earn is spent in four ways. First, the government has mandated us to pay taxes to the IRS before we can pay ourselves. Uncle Sam always takes the first bite, simply because he has first dibs.

Next comes our fixed expenses. These expenses are the rent, house payment, utilities, telephone and more. They are the basics of life which are going to be there every month. We have limited, if any, control over these expenditures once we make a contractual promise to pay.

Our third share goes for variable expenditures. Here is the classic battleground where the war between our wants and our needs is fought. For every need we have, there are usually 744 wants (just kidding). Unfortunately, most people find they have too much month at the end of their money. This is the age old battle of the century. No family is immune. It is at the heart of virtually every family disagreement.

The only way to control the financial battlefield is to have a common goal between spouses. The family that saves together, stays together.

The fourth and final share goes to your investment pool. Assuming you have successfully managed to create a surplus, anything left over at the end of every month should be saved. But where? Some euphemistically call this "share of the pool" savings. Unfortunately,

20

many people often confuse short term savings and long term savings.

TWO TYPES OF SAVINGS PLANS

If you have some savings, where do you put it? In my book, **Baker's Dozen**, I talk about the two types of savings accounts—the "put 'n' take" and the long term savings plan.

A "put 'n' take" is when you put away money for vacations, repairs, appliance purchases and other future expenditures. I find people often delude themselves into believing they are saving. The truth is they are just

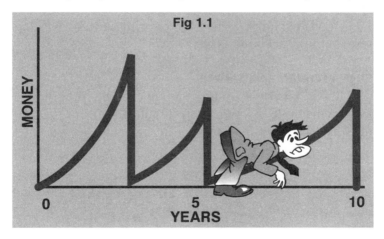

Fig 1.1

deferring. They are deferring their spending. The secret to wealth creation is to NEVER spend capital. The "put 'n' take" is an in-and-out account where the money never stays saved. When you put money into a long term savings account, you must commit to never removing it. You want to let compound interest help you achieve your financial objectives.

Most people are defeated by their "put 'n' take"

account. They put it in and they take it out. They put it in and they take it out. Every time this happens, they "break the chain" of compound interest and must start over. In the appendix of this book is a discussion on compound interest. I hope you study it. There are several surprises many people fail to fully grasp when they learn about compound interest. If breaking the chain plagues you, then I would suggest you take a break from reading this book and pick up **Baker's Dozen**. Then come back and finish reading **Investment Alchemy**.

Okay, let's suppose you are now on the path to financial independence. You have finally made it over the spending hump. You have managed to create an investment surplus. Money is now pouring into your long term savings account. Now what?

THE MONEY MACHINE

This is where a systematic investment program, a money machine, becomes important. If you can systematically invest your money, you can achieve financial success. But if you have no system, you are doomed to

accumulate by chance. A system will beat chance every time. It is the equivalent to the tortoise and the hare. The hare was razzle dazzle and flashy, but did he win? Very few will consistently win by taking chances. There was a study conducted at Princeton University to measure the wealth in America. Researchers discovered 2% of the population were wealthy, by any definition. Another 3% were financially independent. Another 13% had too much month at the end of their money.

The final 82% were dependent upon government programs and family for their financial and retirement security. They either had no system or they had no savings, or both. But you can beat those percentages simply by adopting a plan and then working your plan over an extended period of time.

Let me share the system I have used successfully for many years.

THE BUCKET SYSTEM

To explain how this system works, envision the beach. There you are sitting on the sand with two buckets, one larger than the other. You fill the large one with sand and begin to pour the sand from the large one into the smaller one. What will happen? The sand will build up in the bucket and then eventually, the sand will overflow the smaller bucket and cascade over the side back onto the beach. If you

had a series of these buckets, the sand will overflow the first bucket and pour into the second bucket and then ultimately flow into a third bucket.

That's the way your financial system should work. Fill up the first bucket (your long term savings). When it is full, then let the money flow into the second bucket and finally into the third bucket. Each bucket represents specific levels of risk, rate of return and liquidity. We will look specifically at the types of investments you might select for your buckets in a later chapter. So, let's stay conceptual for now.

THE FIRST BUCKET

Bucket ONE, the first level, must hold investments consistent with long term savings. The risk, liquidity and rate of return associated with the first bucket should be conservative and risk free. For instance, in level one, the rate of return is typically 3% plus the current rate of inflation. Historically, the intrinsic value of money has been 3%. Why? Because 3%, through the years, has been the long term rate of return on low risk, high quality bonds. The interest on bonds represents what people are willing to pay to rent money.

Risk	*None*
ROR	*3% + Inflation*
Liquidity	*High*

Money never deserves a wage, it only deserves rent.

24

Human ability should be rewarded for creating value. Money is only a vehicle. Earnings greater than the intrinsic value of money (the rent—3%) must be attributed to "man at work." In Bucket ONE there should be minimal risk and high liquidity.

What investments reflect the intrinsic value of money? Can you think of any which fit this description? Perhaps a savings account, money market account, CDs, life insurance cash values or special fixed annuities? All of these types of investment fit Bucket ONE.

THE SECOND BUCKET

Bucket TWO should hold investments which reward risk. These securities will have a higher expected rate of return than Bucket ONE—say inflation + 5%-7%. The risk should be moderate and the liquidity should be high. Investments at this level would include stable, long term growth-oriented mutual funds, variable annuities, tax free municipal bonds, conservative individual stocks and bonds. The point is, these assets are fundamentally long term investments designed to take maximum advantage of compounding growth. This portfolio derives its economic advantage from a buy and hold philosophy—which should produce long term growth. You should have an investment horizon of at least five years. Preferably, you would have a 10 to 20 year investment period to maximize the benefits from these vehicles.

Risk — Moderate
ROR — Medium
Liquidity — High

Bucket ONE is the foundation for a successful investment program. The primary objective is long term security and preservation of capital. There is virtually no risk and total liquidity. Bucket TWO holds investment capital that exceeds your current need for security and preservation. The primary objective of this bucket is to take advantage of compound growth over a long time period.

THE THIRD BUCKET

Bucket THREE builds wealth by taking inordinate

risk. The laws of economic growth reward risk, but penalize failure. The risk/reward process takes into account the investor's willingness to "go for it." Sometimes you win and sometimes you lose. Contrast this bucket to Bucket ONE. In bucket THREE man earns value by understanding risk and accepting the potential loss associated with the risk.

Bucket THREE holds what I call "frozen assets." The rate of return could be astronomical or a complete loss. The liquidity is non-existent and the risk is very high. This level includes real estate, business ventures, new stock issues, commodities and a plethora of investment schemes dreamed up by the mind of man. It may take a long time to get your money back. Talk to virtually anyone who has invested in Bucket THREE and he will tell you it can be a money pit. You are likely not to see your money again for at least 10 to 15 years and you may be required to put up significant additional capital to protect your investment because things "just didn't work out."

GOING FOR THE HOME RUN

Before we go on, let me make a couple of observations. It has been my experience that most people who are just starting to accumulate money gravitate to Bucket THREE. Why? Because they are driven by a desire to "strike it rich" and earn the highest rate of return possible, as soon as possible. They see Bucket THREE as the fastest avenue to their financial success. As a result, they unwisely choose a frozen asset. When it doesn't work out and they lose everything, they become more conservative and eventually end up shoving all of their money into Bucket ONE. It is this "hot stove" syndrome which defeats many potential investors. Once burned, most people will not willingly return to the fire.

I find greed to be a "funny" human character trait. When a person first contemplates making an investment, do they ever consider it might be a bad one? I don't think so. Imagine an investor saying this to his wonderful wife. "Martha, I want to tell you about this great investment I just made for you and me. I put our entire nest egg into this bad little investment I heard about. I know this sounds silly, but we are guaranteed we will lose our investment in three years. And the best part is if it really fails, we may have to put more in it to save our house. Isn't that just wonderful?"

Can you imagine ever saying that? Nobody ever invests with the idea he is going to lose money. In fact, it is just the opposite. People have wild dreams of success. I remember when I invested in my first and only oil well. When it hit, I literally dreamed of earning $5,000 per month for life. The first month, I got a check for $2,000 with expectations of more to come. The next month, the check was for $500 and then it finally leveled out at $49 a month for five years. My wide-eyed enthusiasm was reduced to reality—from 100-0 mph, mentally, in two seconds. Then the brakes locked and I went into a tailspin. Was I greedy or just naive? Well, at least I got my money back.

My point is this. Nobody invests with the idea he is going to lose his money. Here's a theory for you. "When someone is making an investment decision, there is no such thing as a bad investment." If you assume all of the economic factors are accurately assessed in your venture, there are really only two ways you can lose your money: you could be defrauded or changes in the economic factors could cause you to run out of time. In either case, the investment could require you to invest more capital than you ever planned or it might require you to make payments you can't afford. You are more likely to abandon the investment (with some debt owing) or you will sell at a loss (if you are lucky). In most cases, you lose your investment entirely. So it is no wonder people become skeptical after losing capital and pull back from Bucket THREE to Bucket ONE. The key to the Bucket THREE is what I call "Staying Power." You need enough extra capital to protect your investment. Why?

TWO BASIC RULES FOR INVESTMENT

Investing is much like science. There are immutable rules, just like gravity and centrifugal force. I think there are two basic rules for investing. First, it is "an absolute sin" to lose capital. This may seem obvious. But how many people have violated it? If you have staying power, you can protect your initial investment until the economic factors turn in your favor. Without staying power, you run the risk of breaking the chain of compound interest. The second rule is even more basic—don't invest money you can't afford to lose. If losing your money will dramatically impact your standard of living or make you uncomfortable, you are making a terrible mistake by investing in something where a loss is possible. Follow your instincts—they are rarely wrong.

HOW MUCH SHOULD BE IN EACH BUCKET?

The amount of money you allocate to each bucket is purely a personal matter. But there are guidelines which can help you make these decisions. Eliot Janeway, a well-known economist from the '60s and '70s, once said that most consumers should have at least six months of savings in a secure investment vehicle (Bucket ONE). Other factors might include job stability, the nature of your debts and family oblig-

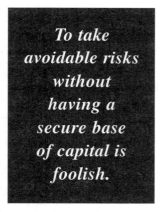

To take avoidable risks without having a secure base of capital is foolish.

ations, as well as your age. The point is, this money should be safe and secure.

The need to assess both your income and your income security is important because there may come unexpected expenditures and emergencies. You also need to inventory your existing "human assets." For instance, if you are earning $100,000 annually in a commission sales job and have no net worth (other than your house), then I think you need to have more in Bucket ONE, say at least $75,000, before you start to venture into the investment arena. This becomes your "staying power."

In today's fast-paced world, change is the norm. Is

there such a thing as a stable job? Technology is changing business practices. To take avoidable risks without having a secure base of capital is foolish. It invites disaster.

It could take you a long time to build up significant Bucket ONE capital. I need to warn you. You will become frustrated when you begin to have too much money in the first bucket. Having $75,000 earning only 4%–5% seems wasteful. But I have seen too many people lose everything because they wanted to earn a greater rate of return on their savings.

Bucket Distribution (Fig. 1.2)

Executive	Variations	1	2	3
A	50,000 Income to 100,000 Net Worth	50,000	50,000	0
B	100,000 Income 500,000 NW	50,000	300,000	150,000
C	100,000 Income 2,000,000 NW	200,000	500,000	1,300,000

The following table may give you an idea of how I would set the Bucket parameters for a salaried executive.

Notice for Executive A, we built $50,000 in Bucket ONE and then built $50,000 in Bucket TWO. I would recommend building another $150,000 in Bucket TWO before even considering an investment in Bucket THREE. You can see this at work for Executive B. In this case, I would suggest having $50,000 in Bucket ONE (6 months income); $300,000 in Bucket TWO and then start building Bucket THREE. There is NO MANDATE which says you must have money in THREE.

Suppose Executive C had a net worth of $2,000,000.

Having $200,000 in a secure savings vehicle would not bother you. But if $200,000 is all the money you have ever accumulated, then you may be tempted to make it work harder for you. Please don't fall victim to this temptation. Remember, 95% of the people do not know how to save or invest. If you vary from this system, you run the risk of losing it all. Then, when you start all over again at an older age, your enemy will become "too little time". It is not worth it.

Let's go back to our $50,000 Executive A. He has a stable job with $100,000 in assets (excluding home). Here he might want to keep $50,000 in Bucket ONE and then put the other $50,000 into Bucket TWO. But as you add more money to the system, where would you place it? I think you should put it in Bucket TWO! Remember, you only go into Bucket THREE when you have completely filled Bucket ONE and TWO. After you hit your goal for Bucket TWO, then you can start putting money into Bucket THREE. Eventually you might want to target $200,000–$300,000 in Bucket TWO before you start thinking about Bucket THREE.

WHAT'S THE POINT?

The point is: this system is very fluid and flexible. It can meet your objectives as you earn more and save more. The key is to develop the savings discipline and develop targets in each bucket. I can virtually guarantee that if you build a personal savings discipline, you will avoid the 82% problem. You will be one of the few who are financially independent at retirement. If you can achieve your objectives along the way, you can obtain financial freedom. The secret is to allow compound interest to help you along the way. The only question is how long will it take you?

I've met families who have several children, a reasonable income ($60,000) and have fully paid off their home with money in the bank. It is wonderful to see how they work and manage their finances. I also have seen families who make substantially more monthly income but have nothing to show for it. The choice is yours. All you have to do is be disciplined with your money.

That's the system. It is very simple, really. Just fill the buckets and let the money flow! Keep adjusting the size of the buckets as you accumulate more and more capital. You can use any system you like, but you must use a system. Once you have money to invest in Bucket TWO, then start to decide which Bucket TWO investments you are going to choose. That's what the rest of this book is about—picking Bucket TWO investments.

Before we look specifically at these Bucket strategies, I want to review how much you really need to have at retirement.

2
The WHATs of Financial Planning

Now that you have created your buckets and allocated your existing assets, let's look at your buckets from a different perspective. I mentioned in the introduction "core" dollars. These are the dollars you do not want to risk. These are the dollars you want to protect under all circumstances. Your "core" dollars should be Bucket ONE dollars and probably most of Bucket TWO. Chances are you would not want to lose money in either of those buckets.

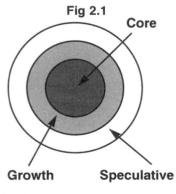

Fig 2.1

Core

Growth

Speculative

Once you have established your core dollars, you then proceed to build your growth dollars. These dollars would be managed with a different investment philosophy. It is important to understand you can keep all of your dollars as core dollars. Nothing says you have to venture out beyond your core. But I find many successful people feel they can do better than simply implementing a core strategy. They feel they can bring the same level of expertise to investing that they brought to their career or business. As a result, they want the joy of picking the investments and managing the process. Why not? After all, it is their money.

WHAT MONEY SHOULD YOU RISK?

I learned early in my financial life, it is far more desirable to play with my profit than with my capital. I like to keep my capital safe and then, if necessary, take "the money that money makes" and gamble on my investment ability. If you can protect your capital, you can afford to take more risk with your profit. As an aside, that's one of the good things about purchasing life insurance and disability insurance. By passing the risk to an insurance carrier, it gives you the peace of mind and security to take greater risks.

I talked to one investor who told me he had matched his personal investment portfolio against his wife's professionally managed one. He let the wizards run with their concepts and he managed his without "looking" at their selections. He then shared with me that he had successfully out-performed the wizards consistently for the last five years. But he also added, he would never want to do this for a living.

I have met many people similar to him. They have experienced excellent short run results, but in their heart of hearts, they know they cannot sustain these results. Look at active money managers! Very few have been consistently excellent over long time periods, according to performance studies. Over the last 20 years, virtually 70% of the active money managers have been unable to consistently outperform the market averages. In recent years, 85% have failed to beat the markets.

When I was a kid, I became interested in horse racing. I read the racing forms and the race results in the daily paper. I would place my imaginary bets and wait for the results the next day. I was a genius. I parlayed my winnings and became the master of the track. However, this was true only on paper. When I finally got a chance to do it for real, I failed miserably. I couldn't risk real money the same way. What was the difference? I think doing the real thing is always harder. It is easy to win when there is no pressure. But when it's your money and you have it on the line, the risk is much different.

Should a person invest his own money? Why not? Especially, if he feels like being involved. But when you can get professional management for a small cost, why risk investing your core money yourself? Let the experts manage your core money. You can play around with some of your growth money and manage the third bucket (the speculative ring).

Speculative investments are generally reserved for those who can afford to lose their money. When you have money in Bucket THREE, you can afford to take a chance—buy a new stock issue, invest in a gold mine, silver mine, etc. Unfortunately, for the most part, long-term speculation virtually guarantees loss. It is the equivalent of buying a lottery ticket. But who knows? That's what is so exciting about it for some people.

If you invest with people you know, who have a proven track record, you might hit a "home run"— it could happen to you. But do you want to risk your core dollars? I don't think so. Well then, do you want to risk your growth dollars? Probably not! So, you need to fill up those buckets and make certain you are well on your way to achieving your financial goals. How many people do you know who want to reach retirement, only to discover they have a reduced standard of living?

If you knew that the ability to have a relaxed and secure lifestyle at age 60 was based on whether or not you lost the money you just invested in that silver mine in Colorado, what would you do? Most of us would pull the money back. Yet, too often, it is only hindsight which is 20/20, not our foresight. It is hard to be disciplined and say "no." It sounds so good. I have a real hunch on this one. I'd hate to miss this one if it really hits.

Just remember, there are probably a million people out there whose whole goal in life is to make you wealthy. (A little sarcasm here.) Why? Because they love you? I don't think so. They want to use your money to fulfill their dreams. They want to get wealthy off your money, while you take all of the risk. If this was such a great investment, why are they willing to share it with you? Why wouldn't they be putting all of their money into it? Logic is not easy when it comes to assessing the "get rich quick" schemes. Once the financial adrenaline starts to boil, it is hard to turn around and go the other way.

What is really funny is who falls for these schemes. It is usually a conservative family who would never waste money on a vacation to Europe or buy an expensive automobile. They are diligent savers and frugal investors. But then, they get suckered into believing the proposed investment is their ticket to the "American Dream." It is almost a lottery mentality. They believe it can happen to them. But the true "American Dream" is based on hard work. Nobody has ever given anybody anything in this country. Instead, most wealth has been accumulated by letting money sit for a long time while it compounds, usually through innovation and technology. I am not trying to discourage anyone from making a good investment. I am simply saying that we need to have a plan, a system.

Wealth is almost never the result of a windfall profit-taking. Easy come, easy go! Wealth occurs when capital or effort compounds for 20 or 30 years. Review the Rule of 72 and the appendix on compound interest to see how long it takes for $1 to become $2. Look how long it takes $2 to become $4 and so on. These intervals (Fig. 2.2) are the key to compound success. Ask your-

Fig. 2.2

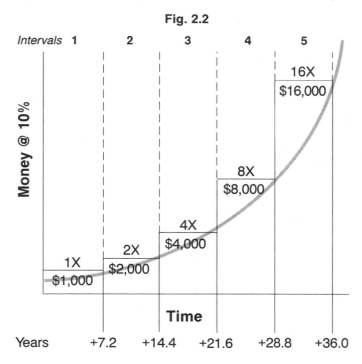

self, how many intervals do you have left between now and retirement?

FIVE KEY QUESTIONS

Enough of this problem, already. I hope it is abundantly clear that everybody needs to protect their core dollars. If you want to reach retirement with $1,000,000 in your core investment vehicles, you need to assess these five questions.

1. **What** risk are you willing to take?
2. **What** capital do you have today?
3. **What** rate of savings will you add to your capital?
4. **What** period of time do you have left to accomplish your objectives?
5. **What** factors will impede your progress?

We call these questions the WHATs of Financial Planning. If you can get a handle on these factors, you can project what results you need to achieve. You can also project your expected results based on an array of carefully defined assumptions.

We have developed a software program called the "WHATs of Financial Planning." This software can help you determine the projected results you must attain to meet your retirement objectives if you don't do anything different. Then, the software will help you measure how much is required to attain your objectives if you stayed on your current path. It also tells you what path you need to take to meet your expectations.

Let's look at each of these factors and make certain you understand why they are so important.

The WHATS of Financial Planning

1. What risk are you willing to take?

This question speaks to the entire issue of your risk tolerance. In the next chapter entitled, "Measure the Risk" I go into the entire subject of risk tolerance. If you can't sleep at night because you are so worried about your investments, then your money is in the wrong place. Your core money is your sleep money. You need to feel confident. Regardless of what happens to the economy, you need to feel safe and secure financially. If you don't feel this way, then you need to reassess your investment strategy. The job of a financial planner is to help you assess your risk tolerance and place you in the best investment strategy for you.

> *The job of a financial planner is to help you assess your risk tolerance...*

2. What capital do you have today?

Obviously, you need to determine where you have your money invested today. You need to allocate your current portfolio into the three buckets. If you have a home, then the value of the home should not be included in any of the buckets. Why? It is likely your equity will always be required to provide your housing. Obviously, if you plan to downsize your living requirements, a substantial amount of the equity will be available for investment purposes. You need to adjust the model to reflect the additional capital.

3. What rate of savings will you be able to add to your capital?

Now comes the magic! Determine how much you are

going to be able to add to your portfolio each year. This is the key to achieving your objectives. You may already have enough money and if it is managed properly, you will make your goal. But if this is not the case, then we have to find a way for you to add to your portfolio.

4. What period of time do you have left to accomplish your objective?

When do you want to retire? This is a significant factor in your planning. How many intervals do you have left? (See the Appendix on compound interest). This is often referred to as your time horizon. But don't be fooled. If you are 60 and you want to retire at 65, your time horizon is NOT 5 years. At age 60, you are likely to live another 20 years. You must manage for the entire term of your retirement as well as the time horizon of your spouse or significant other. There may be, in fact, a 30-40 year horizon if you are 60. If you are 40, the time horizon could be 50 years. So the answer to this question will be quite critical.

5. What factors will impede your progress?

Now that we have the facts, let's look at the road blocks. We have already talked about one— inflation. If you need $1,000,000 in today's purchasing power, how much do you need if your purchasing power drops 50%? You need at least $2,000,000 at age 65 and a heck of a lot more if you live until 90. So we have to calculate not only the drop in purchasing power between now and retirement, but also the continuing decline throughout retirement. If you decide you want to spend capital, the amount you need is less, but not significantly. Also, you must then deal with the issue of outliving your capital.

The other big factor is taxes. It is one thing to calculate how much capital you need, but another important factor which governs your results is how much tax you will pay. Some investments are taxed more heavily than others. Some investments vehicles grow tax deferred, until you take the money out.

A final factor which can inhibit your results is fear. Beware. Fear can stop you in your tracks, prevent you from taking action, cause you to do the wrong thing. Fear and emotion are the enemy of successful investing. A system is your ally. Don't fall victim to the something-is-better-than-nothing mind set. While taking a loss and running away may seem to be the wisest move, it could also spell disaster long term. Look at what happened in 1987 when the market fell 20%. Within weeks it had recovered. The same was true in 1997. The market also eventually recovered from the depression in 1929. If you have a plan, a system and you work it long term, the statistical probabilities are in your favor.

Suffice to say, these five WHATs will have a significant impact on the way you determine your long term plan. I feel strongly that you must have an accurate target to hit. If you are unable to hit your target, then you need to know now, so you can take evasive action. Either way, the accuracy of the information and projections will be based on how well you answer these questions and how well your program performs over the accumulation period.

In the next chapter, we will look at strategies which can reduce your volatility and improve your portfolio's performance.

3
Measuring Risk

Chemical alchemy occurs when you mix many different elements to create a precious metal. Centuries ago, this was seen as voodoo and witchcraft. Today, it is called chemistry. **Investment Alchemy** occurs when you mix key financial principles together to create a successful investment portfolio. Wouldn't it be great if you knew you had a very reasonable chance to achieve your long term investment objectives? Wouldn't it be better if you could do this and reduce your overall risk? **Investment Alchemy** cannot guarantee any results. But by combining widely researched and well-known financial principles, we feel you can significantly increase your probability of accomplishing your investment objectives.

DEFINE YOUR PATH

The path for achieving any objective is clear. You must first *define* your goal, *establish* a plan, *create* a measuring system for assessing your progress and then *do* it. No one ever accomplishes anything by waiting. It is better to start and adjust than to never start at all. This book is designed to help you start—to begin your journey along the path to financial security.

What is a successful investment, you might ask?

Success is in the "eye" of the beholder. To some, success might mean preserving your capital; to another, success may mean doubling or tripling your rate of investment. Others may define success as achieving a steady growth rate over an extended period of time. To me, financial success means growing my capital to the targeted amount over a long time period.

Each investor must determine his own definition of financial success because this becomes the benchmark he will use to measure his progress. Anything short of the mark may be considered short term failure. Cumulative short term failure means you have set your goal unrealistically or there is something dreadfully wrong with your system. But notice, I said, "...may be considered failure." Failure is also in the "eye" of the beholder. Most good investment programs are destroyed because the investor lacked patience and perseverance to stay the course. They sustained short term failure and assumed it was fatal. Failure is never fatal, just as success is never permanent. The real enemy of any reasonable investment portfolio is volatility *not* risk.

Patience is demonstrated when an investor is willing to stick with his stated plan and not deviate just because the investment "noise" becomes so loud he panics and buys into the fear. Every sophisticated investor knows the market is volatile. It will go up and it will go down. Perseverance results from patience. Instead of changing course when your results are less than you anticipated—instead of selling your investments or pulling out of them entirely—hold your position, quiet your fears and stay your course. This is what patience and perseverance are all about. Without perseverance and patience, you are doomed to repeat the mistakes of the past.

WHAT KIND OF INVESTOR ARE YOU?

Another question you must ask has to do with what you basically believe. What kind of investor are you? Look at this matrix and see if you can find yourself. There are basically four generic types of investors: the Guru, the Tactical, the Fundamentalist and the Asset Allocator. Think about it and see if you can determine what you believe to be true.

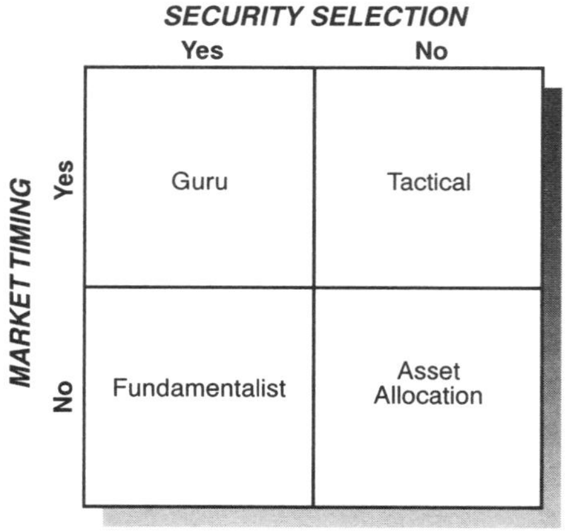

The *Guru* Investor says he believes the market inefficiencies are so great, he can hire an expert who can spot the best deals and also know when the markets are going to turn up and down. Ask yourself, "is it likely anyone can accurately predict the flow of the markets and which stocks to buy?"

Fig. 3.1

SECURITY SELECTION

	Yes	No
Yes	Guru	Tactical
No	Fundamentalist	Asset Allocation

MARKET TIMING

The *Tactical* Investor doesn't believe there are any stock Gurus who can spot bargain buys, but they do believe there are predictable factors which will alert the managers as to when to buy and sell. Ask yourself is it really possible to predict which way the market is going to move? Consistently?

The *Fundamentalist* Investor knows there are no combination of economic factors which consistently predicts market swings, but believes an active manager can consistently spot the best buys and be right a high percentage of the time. These managers will bet on a move in medical or hi tech, for instance. Ask yourself, "Can a stock picker really find bargains in the broad market consistently, especially with the fast pace of information flow in today's world?"

The *Asset Allocation* Investor doesn't believe active managers can be right that often and does not think market turns are predictable. He believes you must pick a strategy and hold on to it for the duration. Ask yourself, "Do you believe a buy and hold position in quality stocks will ultimately attain reasonable and respectable results?"

Patience and perseverance are two elements critical to successful **Investment Alchemy**. Investment Alchemy blends them together. They are the glue which will hold your portfolio in one piece over time.

STAY THE COURSE

So, how do you stay your course? According to most financial analysts, there are three strategies which will give you the highest probability of achieving your financial objectives. Instead of betting on stock picks or market turns, why not rely on a broad based equity selection? Here are the three critical strategies you must utilize in your financial success equation.

1. Asset Class Selection
2. Asset Class Diversification
3. Asset Class Optimization

Asset Class Selection refers to the many different asset classes from which you can choose. What is an asset class? It is a grouping of like-kind securities possessing the same basic economic characteristics. There are three basic asset classes: cash, ownership in a cor-

Measuring Risk

poration and debt (money which you lend to another entity). Ownership is often called equity or stock. Debt is usually referred to as bonds. However, each of these primary classes can have many sub-classifications.

For instance, you can select growth stocks, income stocks or value stocks. You can also select stocks from various industry sectors. In addition, you can chose international, emerging and domestic stocks. We figure there

Fig. 3.2

1 year's Ending:	Inflation	T- Bills	Long Term Government	U. S. Large Co. Stocks	Small Co. Stocks	Int'l Stocks
12/70	5.5	6.5	12.1	4.0	-15.7	-10.5
12/71	3.4	4.4	13.2	14.3	18.4	31.2
12/72	3.4	3.8	5.7	19.0	-.3	37.6
12/73	8.8	6.9	-1.1	-14.7	-39.0	-14.2
12/74	12.2	8.0	4.4	-26.5	-28.0	-22.1
12/75	7.0	5.8	9.2	37.2	65.7	37.0
12/76	4.8	5.1	16.8	23.8	51.1	3.8
12/77	6.8	5.1	-.7	-7.2	26.8	19.4
12/78	9.0	7.2	-1.2	6.6	25.8	34.3
12/79	13.3	10.4	-1.2	18.4	43.2	6.2
12/80	12.4	11.3	-4.0	32.4	41.9	24.4
12/81	8.9	14.7	1.9	-4.9	-2.7	-1.0
12/82	3.9	10.5	40.4	21.4	24.3	-.8
12/83	3.8	8.8	.7	22.5	33.8	24.6
12/84	4.0	9.8	15.5	6.3	-11.6	7.9
12/85	3.8	7.7	31.0	32.2	26.2	56.7
12/86	1.1	6.1	24.5	18.5	3.5	70.0
12/87	4.4	5.5	-2.7	5.2	-14.2	24.9
12/88	4.4	6.4	9.7	16.8	19.9	28.6
12/89	4.6	8.4	18.1	31.5	8.2	10.8
12/90	6.1	7.8	6.2	-3.2	-28.0	23.2
12/91	3.1	5.6	19.3	30.5	51.6	12.5
12/92	3.0	3.5	9.4	7.7	26.0	-11.8
12/93	2.8	2.9	18.2	10.0	19.9	32.9
12/94	2.7	3.9	-7.8	1.3	-2.3	8.0
12/95	2.7	5.6	31.7	37.4	33.3	11.6
12/96		5.2	-.9	23.0	18.4	6.2
Annualized Return	5.6	6.9	9.3	12.3	11.4	12.9
Growth of One Dollar	$4.10	$6.00	$11.10	$22.80	$18.60	$26.40

46

are at least 50 major asset classifications. We'll discuss asset classes specifically in Chapter 4. The table in Fig. 3.2 shows several asset classes and the historic returns since 1970.

Asset Class Diversification deals with how you blend these various asset classes together into one portfolio. Which asset class do you hold and why? This is an important question which needs a specific answer. If you have all of your "eggs" in one asset class, then your portfolio's performance will be predicated on how well your asset class "of choice" performs. But if you have several different asset classes, it is unlikely all of them will perform the same. If the market turns downward, a single asset class would likely perform poorly because it matches the performance of the market. Several asset classes could cushion the fall. We'll see why in a later section.

Determinants of Portfolio Performance (Fig. 3.3)

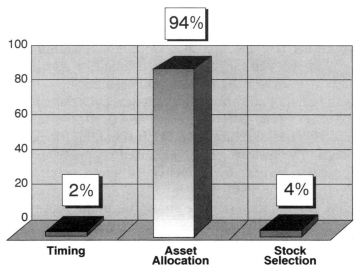

Measuring Risk

A study published in the Financial Analysts Journal in 1986 discussed factors which impact rate of return. The authors determined asset classes accounted for 94% of investment results in the 91 largest pension plans they studied. The other two factors were market timing (2%) and stock selection (4%). This stunning conclusion demonstrates how important asset class diversification really is to your overall portfolio performance. Diversification not only provides a way to protect your entire investment portfolio from disaster, but it also enhances your return. This study suggests asset class diversification is significantly more important than security selection or market timing.

Asset Class Optimization relates to maintaining the best mix of diversified classes for your specific investment profile. Every investor has a risk level which makes them comfortable. Any risk you take beyond your point of risk tolerance will cause severe, major psychological discomfort. An ideal portfolio is based on mixing asset classes in the right combination to meet your risk tolerance profile. Once you determine the level of risk you can stand, you then build a portfolio of asset classes to match this level. Rebalancing refers to maintaining this correct mix of assets over time. Figure 3.4 shows four different asset class portfolios and the historic rates of return for portfolios holding stocks and bonds. The historic yields are based on published performance figures by Dimensional Fund Advisors in Santa Monica, California.

Combining these three strategies, in the proper mix is **Investment Alchemy**. Sustaining your patience and persevering through tough times, are the keys to investment success. But asset classes, class diversification

Annual Returns Jan. 1973 – Dec. 1996 (Fig. 3.4)

	CONSERVATIVE PORTFOLIO	MODERATE PORTFOLIO	GROWTH PORTFOLIO	AGGRESSIVE PORTFOLIO
1/73	1.5	-3.8	-7.8	-12.1
1/74	2.3	-5.5	-12.5	-18.7
1/75	16.4	24.9	32.8	40.0
1/76	13.5	16.7	20.7	24.5
1/77	8.5	13.3	15.4	15.4
1/78	11.7	16.8	19.6	21.2
1/79	12.4	13.9	15.6	17.8
1/80	14.3	17.9	21.3	24.5
1/81	17.5	14.0	10.1	6.3
1/82	21.5	20.6	20.3	19.4
1/83	13.0	17.3	21.1	24.8
1/84	9.9	9.3	9.0	8.3
1/85	21.0	26.9	31.5	36.0
1/86	16.9	21.9	25.1	28.8
1/87	9.2	12.3	14.0	13.0
1/88	11.7	15.9	19.1	22.6
1/89	14.0	19.1	22.0	25.0
1/90	3.6	-1.0	-5.3	-10.0
1/91	15.3	19.4	22.0	26.1
1/92	6.4	6.8	7.1	8.0
1/93	12.3	17.7	20.4	23.6
1/94	-0.0	0.6	1.4	1.8
1/95	11.6	12.9	16.1	19.9
1/96	8.8	10.3	12.1	14.1

and class optimization are only the base "chemicals" for your financial equation. Time is the critical catalyst.

WHAT IS RISK?

I've mentioned the word risk now several times. What is it? Most people think of losing all or most of their money when they hear the word "risk". Well, I think risk refers to the probability of loss. There are two types of loss... loss of capital or loss of income. Your

Measuring Risk

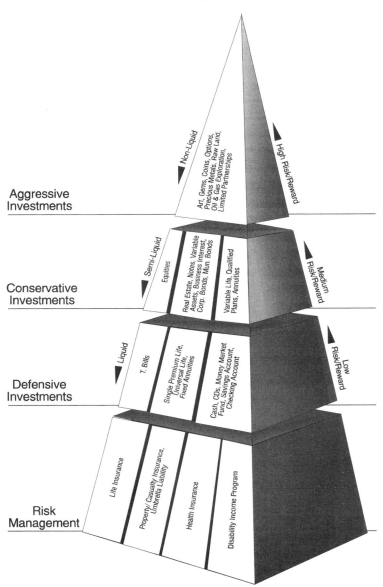

The Risk Pyramid (Fig. 3.5)

ability to recover from loss is often a function of your age, your income potential and how much capital you have accumulated. Why do we invest? For what purpose? Often we invest to create income. Others would say we invest to make our capital grow—money at work. It's not much fun to see your hard-earned capital decline in value. In order to assess the level of risk you are willing to take, you must first assess your objectives. Let's assume you have assessed your objectives accurately and now have a clear understanding of how much capital you need to reach your retirement objectives. Now you must allocate capital to each of your three buckets. There are many relative levels of potential opportunity and probable loss you can choose. Reviewing the Risk Pyramid can give you an idea of different investments you can select. Combining these investments into portfolios—aggressive, conservative and defensive—reflects a wide range of risk choices. Notice an aggressive portfolio does not always rely on stocks to achieve high returns. It tends to have more speculative investments. Growth portfolios have mostly equities which maintain level growth, while conservative portfolios will usually have only low volatility investments. But remember, there are two risks and only one is guaranteed to happen—inflation!

How you decide to structure your portfolio will be based on which risk strata you select and which classes you pick within that portfolio. If you are very conservative, you will likely opt for a lower rate of return—maybe 7%–8% annualized. A moderate strategy might aim at earning 9%–10% annualized. An aggressive strategy would shoot for 12%. A speculative strategy aims to grow at rates way beyond the predictable returns for virtually any asset class. Speculative truly means unpredictable.

Does this suggest you will achieve these targets year end and year out? Probably not! But a conservative strategy is likely to miss the mark by less, year in and year out, than a more aggressive strategy. Why? Because the lower the risk level, the more stable your probable return and the less volatility you can expect to sustain.

VOLATILITY = MOVEMENT

Remember, volatility refers to the movement of the market. Look at the three charts showing stock and bond performance over the last 25 years (Fig 3.6). The annual value of an asset class can fluctuate wildly. By combining a volatile class with a more stable class, the fluctuations are much more modified. The performance becomes more predictable (i.e. Treasury Bonds combined with a small cap or speculative stock fund.) Notice in Fig. 3.7 how much flatter the annual returns are when the portfolio becomes more conservative. Combining varying amounts of C with A and B produces Portfolios D, E and F. Notice E produces a very similar level of risk as

Fig. 3.6

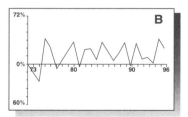

Historical Returns of U.S. Small Cap Stocks 1973-1996

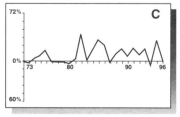

Historical Returns of U.S. Large Cap Stocks 1973-1996

Historical Returns of Treasury Bonds 1973-1996

52

Fig. 3.7

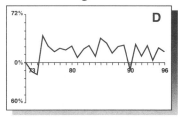

Historical Returns of Aggressive Portfolio 1973-1996

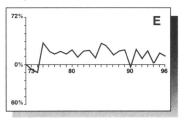

Historical Returns of Growth Portfolio 1973-1996

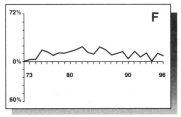

Historical Returns of Conservative Portfolio 1973-1996

C, only with a higher return.

Let's stop here and review the risk principle. What does it really mean to be exposed to risk? Again, most people think risk means the chance or probability of losing all or most of their money. While this could be true, it is true only if you own a small undiversified portfolio of stocks *and* if you happen to be selling your equities at the wrong point in time. If the market goes up, then where was the risk? The risk occurred only when the market was down. Ask yourself this question, "Will the market ever be 'always' down or 'always' up?" Of course not. I prefer to use the term risk to describe volatility—those fluctuations in the value of your portfolio from one measuring period to the next. Most portfolios measure return quarter to quarter.

Moving on, let's look at two different measurements of historic data. The first example (Fig. 3.8) reviews the annual returns from 1973–1996. Look at the high and the low for each asset class during that period and compare the average. The wider the gap, the higher the risk

53

Measuring Risk

One Year Return History 1973–1996 (Fig. 3.8)

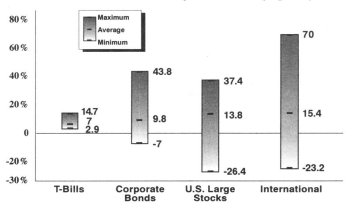

(volatility). But if you had held your portfolio for 25 years, you would have achieved some very good returns for accepting more volatility.

Now, let's look at the same data but use a five year rolling average (Fig. 3.9). A five-year rolling average measures the same historical returns as (Fig. 3.8) but combines them into consecutive five-year groupings. This allows us to factor "staying power" into our model. You'll notice that time has reduced the range between

Full Range Five Year Return History 1973–1996 (Chart 3.9)

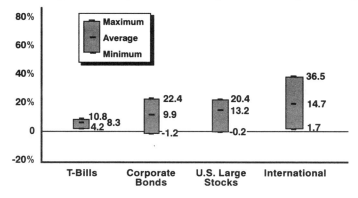

the high and the low, while the average return stayed statistically about the same. Also notice the losses were not nearly as frightening.

Obviously, if you were guaranteed these results today, the decision would be easy. What is not easy is experiencing the "ups" and "downs," the volatility you must endure to obtain these results. This relationship between volatility and return continues to narrow, the longer you hold your portfolio.

WHOSE PRICES ARE THESE?

I am reminded of a story I once heard—a story about measuring risk. A financial advisor went to greet his prospective client in the reception area. When he entered the room, he saw this older gentleman scanning the financial page of the newspaper. After the usual salutations, the advisor asked the gentlemen, "Do you read the financial section of the newspaper every day?"

"Oh certainly, don't all of your clients?" the man responded.

"No, not really," the advisor replied.

"Why do you ask?"

"Oh, I was just curious why you were reading it."

"Well," the investor cleared his throat. "I'm just curious how the market did yesterday and I wanted to see if I made any money on my stocks."

"Were you planning on selling your portfolio, today?" the advisor asked innocently.

"Certainly not, " the investor exclaimed. "I just want to see how my investments did yesterday."

"Whose prices are those listed in that paper?"

"Whose prices? What do you mean?" the investor asked.

"Are those your prices?"

"I'm not sure I understand your question."

"I would like to suggest those stock prices aren't yours. They belong to investors who plan to buy or sell today. Your prices are only quoted on the day you want to trade and not a day before."

Obviously, the point is, unless you are going to sell your stock investments today, those daily quoted values are of no real value to you. They belong to someone else. If you are going to invest for the long run, then you must have a long term attitude. The only time you really need to be concerned about the value of your portfolio is when you are ready to sell.

> *Risk really refers to your ability to liquidate your portfolio for full value at any given point in time.*

I can guarantee you one thing for certain, your portfolio is either going to go up or it is going to go down. But, over the long run, your portfolio should grow at a rate of return consistent with the historical performance of the asset classes you have selected. Risk really refers to your ability to liquidate your portfolio for full value at any given point in time.

THE HOT DOG STRATEGY

Someone once suggested managing an investment portfolio is much like manufacturing hotdogs or sausages. They said if you ever watched hotdogs or sausages being manufactured, you would never eat them. The same is true about the stock market. If you watch your investments too closely, you may get motion sickness. I call this "don't look" money. The best way to be financially successful is to just pick a sound strategy,

U.S. Inflation Growth of One Dollar 1926–1996 (Fig. 3.10)

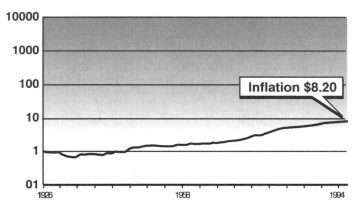

work your strategy over the long run, and don't look at the results until the end. As best I can tell, most of the fortunes made in this country were built from patience. The investor held on to his investment for a long period of time, regardless of the daily ups and downs.

Let's look at what I mean. Using data from Ibbotson, an investment research firm in Chicago, assumes you had invested $1 into an investment which performed exactly like inflation has for the last 70 years. The chart might look like (Fig. 3.10). The inflation rate over the last 70 years has compounded at 2.9%. Your $1 would be equal to $8.20 today.

If at the same time, an investor had selected government securities as their investment medium, they would have earned a compounded rate of return of 3% over the same period (Fig. 3.11). In this case, $1 would now be equal to $34. If the investor had selected corporate bonds as their investment of choice, the historic rate of return for all corporate bonds was 5.7% during the last 70 years. Here, $1 would have equaled $48.

These three assets classes (inflation, government

bonds and corporate securities) are referred to as *loaners*. These investors are lending their money to others for rent (interest).

People who are willing to take risks with their money are often referred to as *owners*. In Fig. 3.12, if an investor would have put $1 into the largest US companies back in 1926 and just let the market ride, their $1 would be worth nearly $1,600 today. That's a historic rate of return of 10.7%. If they would have invested

U.S. Long term Government Bonds and U.S. Corporate Bonds 1926-1996 (Fig. 3.11)

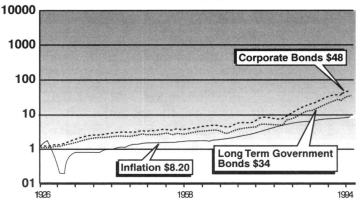

their money in the smallest companies in the market over that same time, their $1 would be equal to nearly $4,000 today, a rate of return of 12.5%.

Think of it. The same $1 invested in loaner investments (debt vehicles) earned between $34 to $48. But the same $1 invested in the equity of America grew between $1,400 in more conservative stocks and over $4,000 in the more aggressive, small stocks. That's quite a difference.

One of the most astute investors of our time, by anyone's standard, has been Warren Buffet. According to

U.S. Small/Large Company Stocks Growth of One Dollar 1926-1996 (Fig.3.12)

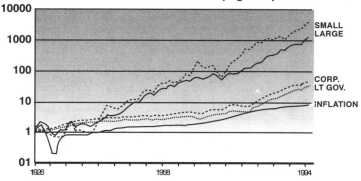

his biography, Mr. Buffet started his investment career buying bargain companies and then selling them once they achieved their anticipated growth level. He then became partners with another man who convinced him to hold on to the stocks and not sell them. This theory was based on the benefits of not incurring the tax every time you sell your gains. Virtually everyone knows the result of Buffet's strategy. He became one of the richest men in the world.

You can attain an equivalent level of success, even though you may never become the richest person in America. All you have to do is buy and hold. Let the market carry you to your objective. You just have to have enough money in your portfolio to achieve adequate diversification and then "stay the course."

RISK = VOLATILITY

Remember, risk only means volatility. Volatility is measured in percentage terms. It is based on how various asset classes fluctuate above and below the average growth rate. Each asset class has a unique historic range of returns measured over a specified time period

Volatility Reduced Over Time U.S. Large Company 1973–1996 (Fig 3.13)

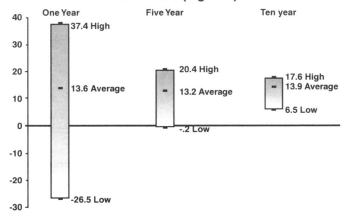

(Fig 3.13). Loss is only realized when you sell. If you "stay the course" for the long term i.e. never sell, history has proven your money will eventually grow. The range of volatility measured annually between 1973 and 1996 ranged between 37.4% and -26.5%. Yet, the average was 13.6%. If you agreed to hold for any five year period, the range of risk dropped to between 20.4% and -0.2%. A 10 year hold was between a high of 17.6% to a low of 6.5%. Note the average return remains virtually the same. (Understand, I am not speaking about any specific investment vehicles—IRA's, annuities, etc—I am speaking only of how a broad portfolio of large stocks as a whole have performed.)

WHAT ARE MUTUAL FUNDS?

Mutual funds have been one of the most popular forms of investment for the "little guy" for several decades. It is a simple, yet effective way to purchase a diversified portfolio of selected investments with a small amount of capital. You have probably seen many of the monthly financial magazines which tout the "hot" fund of the week. Even the local newspapers play this game. These publications rank the funds regularly, using their own criteria, to "help" readers select the best funds for their investments. Their appeal is to the naive investor who believes he can "chase" yield. Some investors think they can anticipate which funds are going to do better than others. Trillions of dollars have been invested in funds, but by a relatively small percentage of the population.

Mutual funds pool together capital invested by individuals, pension plans and other entities. This enables them to own stock in many different corporations at the same time. In some cases, the investors can afford only to own a fractional share of each security. It would be virtually impossible for someone to own .67 shares in IBM, except through a mutual fund. Not only would the expenses associated with purchasing a share of stock be very high, but you would also be required to purchase a minimum number of shares (usually 10 shares).

A mutual fund allows you to spread your risk among all of the investments held by the fund. You would own a fractional interest in every stock held. Now, this is true diversification. If you decided to invest $10,000 in the stock market and the purchase limitation was $100 of stock as a minimum (or at least one full share), maybe you could own 100 different companies. This is effectively impossible because of trading costs. Which of the more than 14,000 stocks would you pick?

The S&P 500 has 500 stocks based on the assets of the largest U.S. companies. The Dow Jones has 30 stocks chosen from the industrial stocks in America. The stock market, as a whole, has more than 14,000 stocks from which to choose. The New York Stock Exchange has approximately 3,000 stocks, the American Stock Exchange has nearly 1,000 stocks and the NASDAQ over-the-counter Exchange has access to 5,000-10,000 stocks. In addition, there are thousands of international stocks, as well. Which criteria or strategy should you use?

You could try picking the fastest growing stocks in the market, the highest dividend paying stocks, the stocks with the largest assets (referred to as capitalization), etc. There are many different strategies you could elect to use. But once you picked your stocks, you would then have to deal with the paper, the taxes and the accounting records. Think of the paperwork involved in keeping track of your portfolio and the tax filing complications when you went to sell some of your stocks! I know, I have done this record keeping for my mother.

A mutual fund allows the investor to make one purchase and own perhaps 1,000 different stocks, all in one account. Mutual funds will differ by how many stocks it holds, what mix, which industry, etc. in the portfolio. These investment decisions depend upon the stated fund objectives, the strategic decisions made by the portfolio manager and the direction of the market. Some investors will decide to purchase more than one mutual fund. Say, for instance, you decided to purchase 10 different mutual funds. You might then own 500 stocks in each of 10 mutual funds. This would be a type of diversification, especially if each fund had a different strategic philosophy.

Now that we have reviewed how a mutual fund allows an investor to purchase many different securities with a small amount of capital, let's look again at whether the stock market is a good place to put your capital. (Remember the two risks—loss of capital and inflation—and only one is guaranteed to happen.)

PREDICTABILITY OF STOCKS

To best understand managing risk, we need to take some time here to learn how predictable the performance of the U.S. stock market has been over the last 70 years. Understand, the market is unpredictable. Yet, I think we have learned that within the chaos is order. While the market is unpredictable, segments of the market have been predictable over time.

The best measure of the U.S. market's long term performance is the Standard and Poor's 500 Index (S&P 500). This index has marked the historic performance of the largest 500 stocks in America, during the last 70 years. Although the actual stocks have varied, the index has remained relatively stable. Fig. 3.14 depicts the historic returns dating to 1926. The historical average return has been 12.7%.

If you measure the average rate of return earned by the S&P 500 over rolling 20 year periods (Fig. 3.15) dur-

Historic Annual Returns and Average Return of U.S. Large Cap Stocks 1926-1996 (Fig. 3.14)

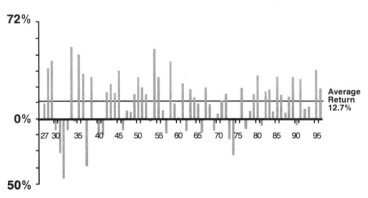

63

ing the last 71 years, it is 10.8%.
There are fifty-two, 20-year periods, during the last 71 years. The
predictability of earning a 10.8%
return over any 20 year period during the past 71 years is plus or
minus 3.3. This was true 67% of
the time, meaning 2/3rds of the
time, the worst you did was earn
7.8% and the best you did was
13.8%. This 2/3rds measure is
called the first standard deviation
in statistics. Most investors would
accept this performance, especially
if it were guaranteed.

WHAT IS A STANDARD DEVIATION?

If you look at the long term
performance of a mutual fund
(assuming it actually has a record
of long term performance), there
should be a measurable average
growth rate over a specified period of time. As I mentioned, statistically, the average annual growth
rate for the S&P 500 over the last
20 years is approximately 12.7%.
This is called an average annual
return. In any given year, it has
been higher or lower than 12.7%,
depending upon which year you
examine. But over the long run,
12.7% is the average annual rate

Fig. 3.15

S&P 500 Twenty Year Rolling Returns	
1/26-12/45	7.1
1/27-12/46	6.1
1/28-12/47	4.7
1/29-12/48	3.7
1/30-12/49	4.5
1/31-12/50	7.4
1/32-12/51	11.7
1/33-12/52	13.2
1/34-12/53	10.7
1/35-12/54	13.1
1/36-12/55	12.5
1/37-12/56	11.2
1/38-12/57	13.0
1/39-12/58	13.5
1/40-12/59	14.1
1/41-12/60	14.8
1/42-12/61	16.9
1/43-12/62	15.2
1/44-12/63	15.1
1/45-12/64	14.9
1/46-12/65	13.8
1/47-12/66	13.7
1/48-12/67	14.6
1/49-12/68	14.9
1/50-12/69	13.4
1/51-12/70	12.1
1/52-12/71	11.6
1/53-12/72	11.7
1/54-12/73	10.9
1/55-12/74	6.9
1/56-12/75	7.1
1/57-12/76	7.9
1/58-12/77	8.1
1/59-12/78	6.5
1/60-12/79	6.8
1/61-12/80	8.3
1/62-12/81	6.8
1/63-12/82	8.3
1/64-12/83	8.3
1/65-12/84	7.8
1/66-12/85	8.7
1/67-12/86	10.2
1/68-12/87	9.3
1/69-12/88	9.5
1/70-12/89	11.6
1/71-12/90	11.2
1/72-12/91	11.9
1/73-12/92	11.3
1/74-12/93	12.8
1/75-12/94	14.6
1/76-12/95	14.6
1/77-12/96	14.6

of return for the general market during the last 71 years. So, let's assume 12.7% is an accurate benchmark.

If in one year the S&P grew only 10%, it was 2.7% below the average of 12.7%. Let's say in another year, the return was 15%, then we could say it was 2.3% above the average. So, by going back into history, we can determine exactly how much the performance varied each year, above or below the average for any class of securities (i.e. small cap, large cap, etc.). By charting all of the returns for the S&P, we can determine the annual fluctuation above and below the average for each year. Historically, this fluctuation was ± 20.3 for the S&P 500 (Fig. 3.16) for any one year period using data which dates back to 1926.

HOW MUCH RISK ARE YOU WILLING TO TAKE?

Again, this statistical measure (the ± 20.3) is called the standard deviation. It measures the most likely range

Historic Annual Returns, Average Return and Standard Deviation of U.S. Large Cap Stocks 1926-1996 (Fig. 3.16)

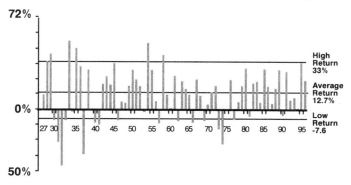

of returns surrounding the average, 2/3rds of the time. For instance, if the returns fluctuated no more than 20.3 above the average and below the average, the expected

return, 2/3rds of the time, would be no more than 33%
and no less than -7.6% (Fig. 3.17). The standard deviation has become a common measure of volatility for the
investment community and a guide to how much relative risk is associated with a specific investment class.
The greater the standard deviation, the more volatility,
as a result, the more risk. (There are other measures of

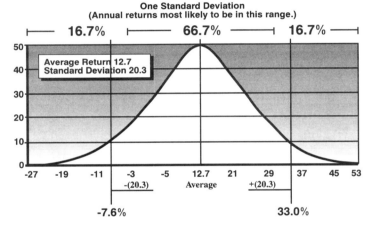

Standard Deviation of the S&P 500 1926–1996 (Fig. 3.17)

risk used by investment analysts, Beta, R2 and the
Sharpe ratios. However, we will not attempt to explain
these in this book.)

How can we use the standard deviation to assess our
risk? First, let's look at how using the standard deviation
compares to the full range of returns. If you refer back
to Fig. 3.2 and 3.4, you'll see the annualized returns for
ALL years. Standard deviation takes into consideration
only 2/3rds of the returns: see Bar (B) in Fig. 3.18. Now,
compare Bar (A) to Bar (B). Bar (B) is the range of
returns within the 1st standard deviation. Notice the
high for all returns is 37.4%, but using (B), the high is

Full Range of Returns Compared with Standard Deviation Returns S&P 500 1973–1996 (Fig. 3.18)

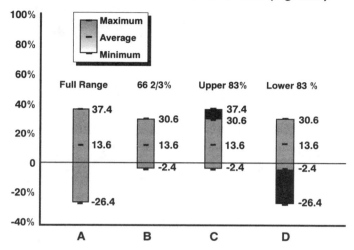

reduced to 30.6%. As you would expect, the highs in Bar (A) are much higher and the lows are much lower.

Look at (C). Notice that these returns include the highs between 30.6% and 37.4%. These returns are outside the standard deviation. The range of returns between -2.4 and 37.4 represents 83% of all occurances (66.7% +16.7%.) That means you only have a 16.7% chance of losing more than -2.4% in any given year. I think it is fair to say, that 83% of the time, your expected returns will be greater than -2.4%.

WHAT'S THE POINT

Why look at Standard Deviation? Asset managers build their portfolios using this key principle of risk measurement. Without it, asset class research would be of less value. It would be difficult to build an effective portfolio. Here are the historic standard deviations for some of the most well-known asset classes for the last

Measuring Risk

Asset Class Standard Deviation, Average Returns and Annualized Returns 1973-1996 (Fig. 3.19)

	ONE YEAR STANDARD DEVIATION	AVERAGE RETURN	ANNUALIZED RETURN
Treasury Bonds	12.9	9.9	9.2
S&P 500 Stock Index	16.7	13.6	12.3
EAFE	22.6	14.4	12.3
U.S. Small Cap Stocks	27.2	16.4	13.0

23 years (Fig. 3.19).

Notice how each asset class has its own distinguishing level of risk. Also, it is important to see the annualized rate of return achieved at each level of risk. We'll see in the next chapter how you can use this information to your advantage.

THE RUBBER MEETS THE ROAD

Let me ask you a question. If I told you most of the time (83%) your investments would earn annual returns between 37.4% and -2.4%, would that be acceptable to you? Could you sleep at night? If you could expect no worse than a -2.4% and no better than a 37.4% gain most of the time, would you be comfortable? Now some people would find this very acceptable. They would trade the probability of a 2.4% loss for the possibility of a 37.4% gain. But others would be scared to death to lose 2.4% and would say, "No thank you," regardless of the upside. What about the other 16.7% of the time? What happens if and when this occurs? That's why risk tolerance is so important. If you think a 2.4% loss is too frightening to tolerate, you need to take a much more conservative approach because 16.7% of the time a bigger loss could occur. But we must remember also that 16.7% of the time, the returns could be greater than 30.6%. The real possibility of losing more than 2.4% in any one year, is limited to only 16.7% of the time.

LETTING TIME REDUCE VOLATILITY

Let's take this a step further in our learning process. Suppose I told you our studies have demonstrated that if you hold on to your investment (no matter what happens) for at least five years, the range of fluctuation of the standard deviation would drop to +8.2. That means most of the time (67%), your portfolio could earn as much as 18.6% and on the low side, it should not earn less than 2.2% (Fig. 3.20). Remember, you still have a 16.7% chance of going lower than 2.2%.

What would you think now? Much better? This is exactly what the historical evidence shows. The longer you hold an asset, the higher the probability it will eventually earn its historical rate of return. This is called

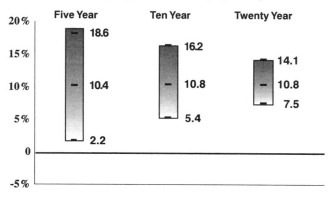

Volatility is Reduced Over Time U. S. Large Company 1926–1996 (Fig. 3.20)

"regression to the mean." Every asset class will eventually perform at or close to its historic rate of return.

Why? I believe it happens because the market is efficient and rewards risk. But it will not over compensate for risk. The proverbial "home run" is made only in extraordinary circumstances. An efficient market will pay only what an investment is worth, over time. "The market does not reward risk which can be diversified away." (*Fortune Magazine* 1/97)

REGRESSION TO THE MEAN

John Bogle, the Chairman and Chief Executive Officer of the Vanguard Group (one of the largest mutu-

One year rank order of top 20 mutual funds out of 681 funds 1982-1992 (Fig. 3.21)

First Year Rank	Average rank in Subsequent Years 83-92	First Year Rank	Average rank in Subsequent Years 83-92
1	100	11	310
2	383	12	262
3	231	13	271
4	343	14	207
5	358	15	271
6	239	16	287
7	220	17	332
8	417	18	348
9	242	19	310
10	330	20	226

al fund families in America, , wrote the book, **Bogle on Mutual Funds**. He determined it is "virtually impossible to pick the winners." Bogle stated, "A passive market strategy will, under all circumstances, past and future alike, outperform the combined results of all active strategies in the aggregate." He also wrote, "The relative return achieved by an equity mutual fund yesterday, has no material predictive value for tomorrow." He then provided the following evidence to demonstrate his point.

Notice the #1 ranked fund, in year 1, (Fig. 3.21) had a 10 year ranking of 100 out of 681 funds. This means although this fund was #1 in 1982, its average rank was 100 after the next nine year period. According to Bogle, the average ranking for the entire group of top 20 funds in 1982 for the subsequent nine years dropped to 284. If you had selected your fund based on who was #1 in 1982, what good would it have done you? One could conclude from this study, that chasing yield is a waste of energy. But to prove Bogle's point further, he went on to rank the top 20 funds for the entire decade from 1972-1982 (Fig. 3.22). He then compared the rankings to the funds' subsequent performance from 1982-1992.

The top ranked fund from 1972-1982 ranked 128th out of 309 funds during the next 10 years from 1982-1992. Note some funds continued to provide excellent performance. But which ones? How can you know?

DECISIONS, DECISIONS

Fig. 3.22

Rank 1972-1982	Rank 1982-1992	Rank 1972-1982	Rank 1982-1992
1	128	11	222
2	34	12	5
3	148	13	118
4	220	14	228
5	16	15	205
7	199	17	209
8	15	18	237
9	177	19	119
10	245	20	242

Measuring Risk

Now we all know blind pigs can find acorns. But, how does a pig know exactly which acorn to pick prospectively? Answer: he doesn't. But in case you are still not convinced. Here's another set of data to consider.

An article in *The Financial Analysts Journal* studied the performance of a random portfolio compared to the benchmark performance of the market. The random portfolio's performance used historic data for identical investment classes. In essence, the authors created a random model, which would be statistically significant. "Statistically significant" means there was enough data to overcome any short term bias caused by bad data. How did they do this? They flipped a coin. Heads you win, tails you win. Except in this case, the investment results of the random portfolio were determined by the heads or tails outcome from 10,000 coin flips.

The coin flip determined the asset allocation mix for each period of the study. If it came up heads, the researchers invested 65% of the assets in the S&P 500 and 35% in treasury bonds. But if it were tails, they reversed it: 35% was invested in the S&P 500; 65% in treasury bonds. The investment results (using actual historic returns for the S&P 500 and treasury bonds) over 60 periods (simulating a rolling five year average) was 12.52%.

How did this compare with actual performance of institutional, active managers? The results were almost identical over the same number of time periods. The spread between the highest percentile and the lowest percentile was 4%. This was virtually the same for the portfolio created in the study. In other words, a random portfolio, using coin flips, performed identically to the market. It mirrored the actual historical fund performance of the active manager. Conclusion:

Active management added no valve to market performance in this study.

PIPER STUDY

Another authority in the field of investment analysis is Piper Analytical. In a study Piper completed on yield regression (Fig. 3.23), they discovered mutual funds, using the same investment objectives, ended up within nearly the same rate of return over an extended time period. In other words, the best funds in the beginning of the analysis, under-performed the other funds, while the

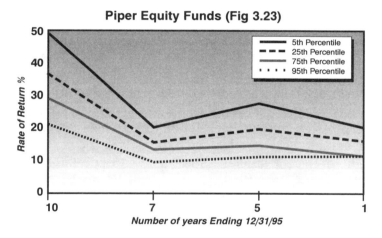

Piper Equity Funds (Fig 3.23)

poorer performing funds, out-performed the early leaders in later years and virtually ended up the same. Time is the great equalizer.

TWO CONCLUSIONS

What might you or any other prudent and rational investor conclude from this information? For me, I have determined two strategies. First, if you are patient, holding your portfolio minimizes volatility (Fig. 3.24).

Measuring Risk

Volatility is Reduced Over Time U.S. Large Company 1926-1996 (Fig. 3.24)

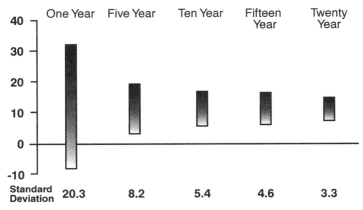

	One Year	Five Year	Ten Year	Fifteen Year	Twenty Year
Standard Deviation	20.3	8.2	5.4	4.6	3.3

Second, because of the efficiencies in market information, most actively managed funds will perform about the same, over time, especially when selecting large company stocks. Today, the U.S. stock market moves so quickly, it is very difficult for an investment manager to obtain a long-term edge and extremely difficult to sustain it. Recent studies show there is opportunity for active management in smaller capitalized stocks. Active managers may have an advantage in small stock and international stocks.

You must ask yourself this question: "If, over the long term, an asset class rate of return is statistically predictable, why should anyone pay larger asset management fees to match or possibly underperform the market?" It does not make sense.

We feel that the longer your time horizon extends, the more likely investing in market-based funds, will sustain the best net returns. So, if you have a long time horizon, the probability of risk (read this as "volatility") actually reduces. The evidence shows, you can reasonably expect the asset class fund to perform according its historical average return over time, especially if you are investing in market-based funds instead of actively managed funds.

Now that we have looked at volatility and regression to the mean, let's see how to *diversify* your investment portfolio.

4
Portfolio Diversification

We have seen the value of holding assets for an extended period of time. Now let's look at the final key to **Investment Alchemy**—the key to successfully obtaining market-based performance. Diversification generally means spreading your risk. There are two ways to spread risk. You can select a wide variety of securities (different stocks and bonds) or you can spread your risk among a wide variety of securities, segregated by distinct asset classes (many securities categorized by a specific criteria). Remember, risk refers to your ability to liquidate your total investment for full value at any given point in time. It is best to think about market risk as volatility. Diversification of risk means spreading your investments in an effort to hold assets with different kinds of risk (economic, interest rate, currency, technological, etc.).

For many years, investors diversified by buying 8-10 different stocks or more. Certainly, holding 8-10 stocks is much better than holding just one stock. But it is not enough to just invest in several different stocks. Historical analysis has shown a market-based return is the best way to attain significant long term performance unless you have a terrific crystal ball. A market-based return is obtained by investing in a portfolio of securities which represent the whole market.

Research has shown you have a much higher probability of achieving an acceptable return if you invest in the market as a whole and not just in specific securities. It is much better to hold thousands of different securities than just 8-10 different quality stocks. We saw in the last chapter why a mutual fund offers a logical solution to diversification. Mutual funds minimize investment expenses. They let you hold a large number of stocks and also allow you to purchase systematically, small incremental shares over time. Mutual funds can also help you accomplish asset class diversification and actually minimize your risk (volatility).

The question which needs to be asked is, "Do you invest in the market as a whole or can you invest in selected segments of the market, based on knowledgeable research?"

WHAT IS DIVERSIFICATION?

Simply put, diversification is spreading your ownership across many different companies (using stocks and/or bonds) to minimize the impact of business problems, business cycles, political events and impact of bad management. The market moves up and down based on a variety of factors and none of these factors are truly predictable. If they were, the professional investors would have already anticipated the moves and purchased or sold the stock. The "little guy" would be left behind. This paradox is what makes the market so fascinating. It is random yet, over time, very predictable. By owning a small amount of stock in a large number of companies, you minimize the impact of these uncontrollable, non-economic factors. (Can you control poor management, political unrest, legislative action aimed at a specific industry or technological change? I don't think so.) Your risk is primarily the uncontrollable economic factors which impact supply and demand (interest rates, value, obsolescence, etc.)

Interest rates tend to track the money supply. They also reflect consumer fears about inflation and unemployment. Value responds to market demand as does obsolescence. Technology may be sweeping or it may be isolated. Consider the printing press and its impact on the information exchange. Suddenly, mankind had access to information as never before. The computer and the Internet are doing the same thing. The Industrial Revolution increased productivity and moved people from the farms to the cities. Today, farmers produce significantly more food with only 1% of the work force. These economic factors positively impact value and consumer confidence.

TWO FORMS OF DIVERSIFICATION

Diversification then is created by spreading your investment into multiple securities. But there are *two* forms of diversification—*efficient* and *inefficient*. Any form of diversification is better than no diversification. But the **goal** of long term investing is to optimize your portfolio for maximum gain and minimum risk of loss. What most people don't know is that inefficient diversification reduces long-term performance and increases volatility in your portfolio.

Before we look specifically at these two forms of diversification, let's look at the history of the market. Investor surveys show an investor's greatest fear is the total loss of capital. Is this fear realistic? Suppose you had invested in U.S. large stocks just before the three worst investment periods we have seen so far—the crash of 1929, the crash of 1973-1974 and the crash of 1987. Even in those stunningly bad years, you would not have lost all of your capital. Look at Fig. 4.1.

Top of the Market Investing (Fig. 4.1)

	1926	1973		1987	
	U.S. Large Company	U.S. Large Company	Diversified Portfolio	U.S. Large Company	Diversified Portfolio
Deposit	$10,000	$10,000	$10,000	$10,000	$10,000
1 Yr Later	$9,200	$8,500	$8,200	$10,500	$10.400
5 Yrs Later	$5,500	$9,900	$17,700	$20,400	$18,500
10 Yrs Later	$9,100	$19,100	$28,900	$41,500	$31,600
20 Yrs Later	$18,400	$85,600	$140,500	?	?
30 Yrs Later	$114,700	?	?	?	?

Most people think of the great depression as the worst period in our economic history. Let's assume some motivating salesperson talked you into putting your $10,000 nest egg into the market on January 1, 1926. Using the Large Company historic returns, let's look back at 1926. Your initial investment would have declined nearly 50% by 1931, five years later. But within 10 years you would have been within 9% of your original investment. Twenty years later, you would have had a little more than $18,000.

Fast forward to 1973 Let's assume you put your $10,000 into U. S. Large Company stocks on November 1st. One year later, you would have lost 15% of your initial investment. But by 1983, (10 years later) your initial investment would have almost doubled to $19,100.

If you had invested $10,000 on October 1, 1987, you would have $10,500 one year later, despite the October crash. By holding your investment for ten years, until

1997, your account would have been worth over $41,500. What's the point? During the worst market declines, nobody lost their initial investment unless they were forced to sell. Worst case, if they had to sell they would have lost 45% of their capital.

So when should you invest? Right now is not soon enough; losing your money is a myth—unless you sell.

I have been making a case for using a diversified portfolio. Suppose you invested your $10,000 into a diversified portfolio instead of just large company stocks. Fig. 4.1 shows what would have happened after the 1973 crash in a diversified portfolio. One year later, your original investment would have been worth $8,200 compared to $8,500. But in 5 years, the portfolio would have more than doubled to $17,700 compared to $9,900.

> *Your risk is primarily the uncontrollable economic factors which impact supply and demand ...*

The crash of 1987 is another time frame to compare the two approaches. In the 10 years since 1987, a diversified portfolio would have underperformed the exceptional "U.S. Large Cap" stock performance during the 90's. However, this is a journey over 30 to 40 years. The key to enduring market volatility is holding an efficiently diversified portfolio for an extended period of time. At any point in time, you may do better with one specific class, but it is unlikely you'll know which class to select. Hindsight is always 20/20.

SIMPLE AND DOUBLE DIVERSIFICATION

Using one asset class is what I call simple diversification. It spreads your risk among many different securities in the same asset class (all growth stocks, all small cap, all large cap). You may own a small number of shares in many different stocks, but they all react to the market in a similar way. Simple diversification is inefficient because by staying in one asset class you have maximized your exposure to market volatility. Beware! Many portfolios using different mutual funds claim to be diversified, but in reality have purchased several funds which are essentially the same asset class. All the investments are in that one class and reflect exactly the same risk in the market.

Double diversification achieves better diversification than simple diversification. It spreads your risk across several asset classes using many specialized funds. We believe "double" diversification can actually enhance your return. How? If you reduce volatility, you enhance the compounding rate of growth. You also benefit from the independent price movement among these classes. The more unique the asset class, the more likely the asset class is to perform independently. This is called *dissimilar* price movement. We will look at this more closely later in this chapter.

OWNERS AND LOANERS

In order to double diversify, we need to understand asset classes. An asset class is a way to categorize various types of securities. In the last chapter, we looked briefly at three basic asset classes—cash, equity and debt. There are arguably several hundred asset classes depending on how you choose to define an asset class. Let's look at some of the basic sub-groups. I am not going to attempt to describe them all; however, it is important to understand the basic concept.

Debt refers to the money borrowed to finance business activity. We've discussed bonds briefly and said they could be considered part of our Bucket TWO investments. Bonds are issued by corporations or government entities to raise money. The interest rate a bond pays is based on the financial strength of the organization and on the public's perception of the financial strength. The stronger the company, the higher the rating and the lower the interest paid to the bondholder. These bonds are bought and sold by investors until they mature. (Maturity occurs when the debt is paid off by retiring the bond and returning the investor's money). Bonds come in various forms. But in all cases they are classified as debt. Somebody is paying you rent for the use of your money. It's just like depositing your money into the bank. The bank is renting your money for a basic wage—we call this wage interest. Earlier, I called people who purchase debt *lenders* or *loaners*.

Equity on the other hand is purchased by owners. Stock equity means ownership of stock. An ownership interest in a business is typically represented by a stock certificate showing the number of outstanding shares of stock you own. You can own tangible property like real estate, or personal property such as a car, furniture, clothes. Owning stock is very intangible. All you have is a piece of paper. The value someone is willing to pay you for the stock is what's important. The price can vary based on the perception of value. The people who have purchased equity are *owners* and they take risk when they own.

COMMON VS. PREFERRED STOCK

As an owner of stock equity, there are primarily two different kinds of stock from which to select—preferred and common. If the corporation is sold or liquidated, the stockholders stand last in line behind everybody else—behind the banks, second-line financing and bondholders—everybody, even the employees.

Common stock stands behind the preferred stock at liquidation, too. It stands last in line. While some common stock might receive a percentage of the company's earnings every year (called dividends), preferred stock is issued with the expectation shareholders will be paid these dividends each year. Investors who are interested mostly in income are willing to sacrifice some future appreciation. They are likely to purchase preferred stocks, which pay significant dividends. Preferred stock does not usually appreciate in value to the same degree as common stock.

Stock prices rise and fall based on the market's perception of its value.

As you can see there are two different ways to infuse additional capital into a company—you can either lend the company money or you can buy its stock and potentially participate in its growth. Common stock is used most often to raise capital because it is the least expensive way to obtain cash. There is no interest owed on the money and the capital never has to be repaid by the company. Common stock has an unlimited upside potential, based on the performance of the company and the market's perception of its value. Preferred stock is rarely used in small growth companies because the dividends reduce the working capital of the company. But, remember with both bonds and stock, it is possible to lose your entire investment if the company goes out of business. This is why spreading your risk through mutual funds is so powerful.

WHY THE MARKETS FLUCTUATE!

Once a corporation issues stock, other investors can offer to purchase the stock on the open market (New York Stock Exchange, NASDAQ, etc.). Stock prices rise and fall based on the market's perception of its value. This perception is determined by the products the company manufactures or distributes, the quality of the management, the sales volume, the earnings per share after all expenses, the book value of the company and the future of the industry or the company, as judged by investors. All these factors combine to create market value.

If the market (the buyers) feels a company possesses a large number of positive attributes, then the market value should rise to reflect a growing optimism. So long as the investors' perceptions are positive, the stock usually retains its market value and may even increase its value as company performance improves.

Once the buyers begin to suspect the company is doing poorly, (sales are falling, inventories are rising, technology is waning)—the buyers will begin to sell at any price to get out.

A stock may fall out of favor and lose value because investors just won't buy it. Stock prices can also decline when "bad news" is reported. When interest rates, inflation rates, and or unemployment rises, investor confidence drops—along with the market. The only way to thrive in the market is to ignore the "noise" and just ride the market through good times and bad times. Nothing is forever.

DOMESTIC OR FOREIGN

World wealth has doubled during the last 20 years. In 1970, the U.S. share of world wealth (Fig. 4.2) was 66%. Today, the U.S. is only 33% of world wealth. Now ask yourself—has the U.S. declined in value? Hardly! Value is being created throughout the world at a startling rate. I believe this growth in world wealth argues for placing some of your investment capital into international funds. The question is how much should an investor risk in the international markets? Remember risk means volatility. The European, Asian and Far Eastern countries (EAFE index) have become very stable in recent years. Even the

The Majority of the World's Equity Markets Have Moved From U.S. to International (Fig. 4.2)

Asian hiccup in late 1997 should not reduce investment opportunity over the long run.

Another opportunity is the emerging geographic areas such as Mexico, USSR, Africa, South America, and the Pacific Rim. These areas can be very volatile, but represent substantial opportunity for investors during the next 20 years.

CAPITALIZATION

Once we divide classes into equity and debt, then into foreign or domestic, we can look at another asset classification—capitalization, the net worth of the company. Capitalization is often broken down into small and large capitalization. If you divide all publicly traded corporations into tenths based on capitalization,

U.S. Small/Large Stocks Highest and Lowest Return (Fig. 4.3)

Low Correlation of Returns Demonstrates Diversification Benefits of Owning Both.

□ The highest decile returns of that year

▨ The lowest decile returns of that year

NYSE Decile	1	2	3	4	5	6	7	8	9	10
1926–28	28.26	25.90	20.56	26.30	19.28	21.41		17.31	21.25	20.84
1929–31	-26.79	-33.06	-35.65	-36.69	-37.13	-39.19	-40.56	-44.77	-49.31	-49.69
1932–34	10.61	23.85	28.86	29.73	20.19	31.19	27.63	41.35	41.23	60.77
1935–37	8.18	9.19	2.29	29.43	8.67	5.36	10.56	3.58	12.48	8.75
1938–40	6.09	4.18	7.06	8.38	12.48	12.87	9.73	8.42	2.44	-8.47
1941–43	7.81	15.31	14.88	15.83	16.79	16.48	24.75	30.31	33.47	55.46
1944–46	13.14	20.83	20.04	24.02	26.64	27.15	25.86	28.90	35.59	38.61
1947–49	9.08	8.24	8.13	6.80	6.35	5.48	3.55	3.85	2.70	4.61
1950–52	21.39	22.71	19.15	20.93	19.15	20.16	21.50	21.81	18.59	18.39
1953–55	24.38	22.12	22.88	22.74	24.38	21.46		20.77	22.81	24.74
1956–58	10.63	15.09	13.03	14.92	10.70	15.41	14.45		15.26	13.18
1959–61	12.49	13.19	15.98	14.40	14.44	13.45	14.41	13.82	14.32	12.76
1962–64	8.25	6.73	6.65	5.63	2.63	3.73	5.12	5.33	3.63	4.46
1965–67	5.96	10.85	16.40	19.58	22.86	25.18	26.15	30.21	33.33	39.51
1968–70	1.26	1.83	-2.30	0.04	0.41	-4.36			-3.70	-3.05
1971–73	7.22	0.82	3.27	-0.34	-3.60	-3.54	-7.42	-10.65	-6.39	-10.01
1974–76	4.19	11.62	13.04	15.90	14.55	14.77	17.17	20.00	19.55	22.46
1977–79	4.59	8.63	13.38	16.87	19.79	22.82	25.26	25.05	27.75	34.74
1980–82	13.47	17.36	19.00	20.07	20.92	22.18	20.17	20.56	20.16	19.41
1983–85	19.06	20.53	18.34	16.96	17.23	19.04	19.52	18.32	16.87	11.94
1986–88	12.32	13.30	13.20	13.04	11.13	8.23	8.39	6.80	3.07	0.74
1989–91	19.44	16.48	18.01	16.52	14.85	13.40	14.44	9.39	8.43	2.26
1992–94	4.62	8.26	9.34	9.07	13.50	12.46	13.02	9.43	11.17	18.31

1/10 of the corporations will be allocated to each decile. The very largest companies would be in decile 1, while the smallest 1/10 of publicly traded companies would be in the 10th decile.

Fig. 4.3 displays the three year rolling returns for all U.S. companies by decile for the last 70 years. For instance, in decile 1, between 1926–1928, these stocks grew 28.26%. However, decile 5 grew the largest, 29.43%, and decile 8 grew the least, 17.31%. Notice where the preponderance of highs and lows are—in deciles 1, 2, 9 and 10. New technology usually incubates in small start up companies. If the technology or research becomes marketable, the company value will grow to reflect investor interest. Many Fortune 500 companies are the result of break through products which are now industry standards. The historical growth of small cap companies has been at a much faster rate than the larger cap firms during the last 50 years. Why? More risk, more opportunity. The market rewards the risk takers.

More importantly, the smaller cap and larger cap companies have historically provided unrelated performance. The price movement of these deciles have been independent of one other. Why is this important? A portfolio needs to have independent price movement of asset classes to benefit from dissimilar price movement. By building a portfolio that matches these two asset classes, we create double diversification. I will show you the value of this later.

The extreme deciles (1, 2 and 9,10) have significantly outperformed the companies in deciles 3-8. If you are seeking top performance, why would you want to invest in mutual funds which hold a large percentage of the their funds in deciles 3-8? Many investors purchase funds which invest in all of the 10 deciles and do not effectively increase growth by doing so.

Fig. 4.4 shows the difference between large cap and small cap stock performance over the last 70 years. Obviously small cap has outperformed large cap, but at what cost? Let's see what risk was associated with the reward. Remember our discussion on standard devia-

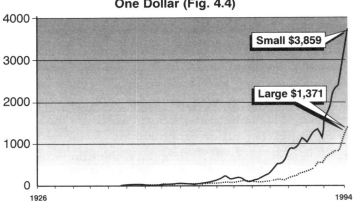

U.S. Small/Large Company Stocks Growth of One Dollar (Fig. 4.4)

tion? Standard deviation measures the variability of return from the average return. The ± for the large cap is 13.9, but the ± for small cap is 23.4. This means you will have a lot more VOLATILITY. Small caps are not for the faint of heart. (This is why there is a greater chance that, in the short run, you will get less of your capital back if you want to liquidate your holdings.) Basic rule—never risk more than you can afford to lose. Remember your sleep factor.

VALUE STOCKS

We have looked at both international and domestic, small and large cap stocks. Another major asset classification is value stocks (Fig. 4.5). Many companies have lost their appeal on Wall Street. The professional money managers are seeking other investment opportunities and these value stocks are no longer the "darlings" they once were among active managers. Even so, they are still stable stocks and good long term investments. Their common characteristic is value. Value means the net worth of the company is very high compared to the price investors are willing to pay.

Value Asset Class—Diversification and Increased Returns (Fig. 4.5)

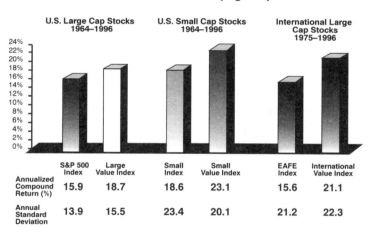

	S&P 500 Index	Large Value Index	Small Index	Small Value Index	EAFE Index	International Value Index
Annualized Compound Return (%)	15.9	18.7	18.6	23.1	15.6	21.1
Annual Standard Deviation	13.9	15.5	23.4	20.1	21.2	22.3

Contrast the performance of growth stocks to value stocks. Most growth companies have a very small net worth. But optimistic buyers are willing to pay a lot for the glowing promise of future sales and profits.

Value stocks have a lot of assets and a profitable product line. They are not likely to fall off the charts and disappear. But they are not going to make any investment manager a superhero, today. It is interesting to note that studies have shown "large cap value" stocks have outperformed growth stocks by as much as 3% over the last 30 years (Fig. 4.5).

A BALANCED PORTFOLIO

All of these assets classes constitute a well-balanced portfolio. By spreading your investment over these classes, you can achieve what I call "double" diversification. Not only are you diversified by having a large number of securities in your portfolio, but you are also diversified because you have a wide range of asset classes which react to market conditions differently. Asset classes perform uniquely, depending on the capitalization of the stock, the geographic location of the companies and the development of the company in the business cycle. Matching the best asset classes within a specific risk profile is accomplished by predetermining the historical rate of return for each class and how each class performs, compared to other asset classes. Statisticians call this comparative relationship "correlation." Each class moves in a statistically significant pattern and can be statistically related to each other.

A significant only problem you must avoid is "style drift." Style drift occurs when money managers make stock selections which "drift" outside of the stated objectives of their fund. If they are a large cap fund and they purchase junk bonds or small cap stocks, they have left their defined style.

For purists, who want to buy asset classes true to the definition, this is unacceptable. Competition and the pressure for higher returns will cause managers to change investment course.

CORRELATION COEFFICIENT

Correlation coefficients measure the relative movement between two or more asset classes over a specified period of time. We've seen from our previous discussion that stocks fluctuate in value. It makes sense that a fund of similar stocks will move in the same manner. Market value for the fund will go up and down based on market forces. But while some classes are going up, other classes are coming down. By analyzing the historic data for each class, a pattern emerges which is statistically measurable. This measurable pattern is expressed as a correlation coefficient and becomes a very important part of portfolio construction.

We have seen how historical data is a predictor of future asset class performance. We can also ascertain how an asset class is likely to react compared to other classes based on market influences. A classic example of this phenomenon is an historic analysis of the EAFE (Europe Asia and Far East) Index and the S&P 500 Index. Fig. 4.6 shows the incremental difference in gain or loss of one index versus the other, year by year. So, if the S&P 500 was up 10% and the EAFE was up 5%, the chart would reflect a +5% difference for the S&P 500. There were periods when the U.S. markets outperformed the EAFE and periods where the EAFE outper-

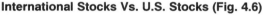

International Stocks Vs. U.S. Stocks (Fig. 4.6)

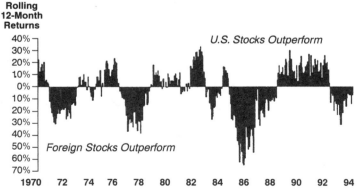

91

formed the U.S. If you made a mistake and invested in the wrong index, your results would have been worse than if you had combined them. This may seem counter intuitive, but by being in both, your long term results would have been less volatile with higher returns than if you tried to pick the best one.

Some asset classes react the same as economic and business factors change. Others are totally independent of each other. If the asset classes have no relationship at all, statisticians say, they have a zero correlation. They are totally independent. The individual investment results are unrelated. Certain classes do move the same way, while other classes move opposite to each other. Figure 4.7 shows some of these relationships.

If two classes move similarly to each other, they are positively correlated. Asset classes which are perfectly correlated will score a +1. If they are perfectly uncorrelated (moving in different directions), they would measure a -1. By knowing the correlation of asset classes, we can build a portfolio which has efficient diversification, through dissimilar price movements.

Our chart (Fig. 4.7) shows that International Small

Correlations Can Range From +1.0 To -1.0 (Fig. 4.7)

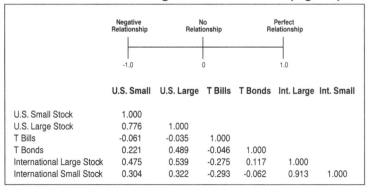

	U.S. Small	U.S. Large	T Bills	T Bonds	Int. Large	Int. Small
U.S. Small Stock	1.000					
U.S. Large Stock	0.776	1.000				
T Bills	-0.061	-0.035	1.000			
T Bonds	0.221	0.489	-0.046	1.000		
International Large Stock	0.475	0.539	-0.275	0.117	1.000	
International Small Stock	0.304	0.322	-0.293	-0.062	0.913	1.000

and International Large are 91.3% correlated. This data suggests both classes have a high probability of moving in the same direction at the same time. By matching these two classes with negatively correlated classes we can potentially eliminate the wide fluctuations associated with either class.

EFFICIENT DIVERSIFICATION

The benefit of efficient diversification is improved long term performance. Let's assume we have only two asset classes—A & B. Look at Fig. 4.8. You'll notice portfolio A has the same rate of return each year (10%). It will yield the same average return as portfolio B, which fluctuated widely.

Now look at Fig. 4.9. Notice the difference in the beginning and ending balances, when you start with $100,000 of initial capital. Portfolio A is worth $259,370, while investment B is worth only $210,260. The wide fluctuations in return caused this loss. The average return does not reflect the actual performance. Be careful when you compare returns. It is easy to confuse annualized and average returns.

Average Return Fig. 4.8

Year	Portfolio A	Portfolio B
1	10	20
2	10	-15
3	10	-10
4	10	20
5	10	35
6	10	-15
7	10	45
8	10	15
9	10	5
10	10	-5
Average	**10%**	**10%**

They are not the same. The average return is the sum of all the returns divided by the number of occurances. The annualized return is time weighted and measures the internal rate of return including the length of the investment period and when the capital was invested.

Losses (wide fluctuations) have a dramatic impact on the compounded rate of return. One of the most important portfolio objectives must be to smooth out these fluctuations. This can be accomplished only by matching asset classes with dissimilar price movements. By using the correlation coefficients, we can blend asset classes and attempt to smooth out the

Growth Fig. 4.9

Year	Portfolio A	Portfolio B
Deposit	100.00	100.00
1	110.00	120.00
2	121.00	102.00
3	133.10	91.80
4	146.41	110.00
5	161.05	148.72
6	177.16	126.41
7	194.87	183.29
8	214.36	210.79
9	235.79	221.33
10	259.37	210.26
Average	10.00%	10.00%
Annualized (IRR)	10.00%	7.71%

ever present volatility. By minimizing the ups and downs of the portfolio, overall performance should improve.

Another way to look at how important this factor can be for your portfolio is to look at what would happen if you selected similar asset classes.

Figure 4.10 is an example of what I call "inefficient diversification." Note both asset classes are moving in the same direction. This is what happens when you invest in similar classes which have the same basic market influences. The only way to avoid inefficient diversification is by matching asset classes with dissimilar price movement.

In order to better illustrate the value of dissimilar price movements, let's look again at the historical performance of S&P 500 and the EAFE (Fig. 4.11). If you were to have invested 100% of your capital in just the U.S. market over the last 20 years, your annualized rate of return would have been 11.3%. If instead, you used the EAFE index, your rate of return would be 15%. But by

Inefficient Diversification (Fig. 4.10)

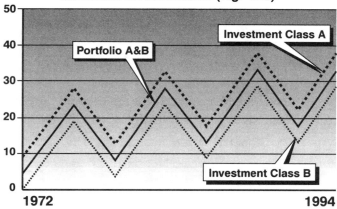

1972   **1994**

combining them, placing 50% in EAFE and 50% in U.S. large, guess what happened. Your combined rate of return was 17%. But more importantly, the standard deviation of risk was actually reduced. In essence, you achieved higher returns and reduced the level of volatility.

When asset class performance moves in opposite directions, the net yield should create a smoother compound growth curve (Fig. 4.12). Assuming the average return is the same over the equivalent time period, the

International Stocks Vs. U.S. Stocks (Fig 4.11)

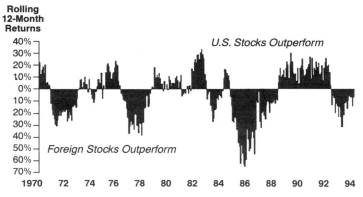

95

result from an effective diversification will be a higher net growth for the overall portfolio.

The primary goal of any asset manager should be to maximize portfolio performance by maximizing return. The goal is best achieved by creating a smooth performance over an extended period of time. Unfortunately, the primary goal of a mutual fund manager is quite different. They seek to maximize the return of the fund in

Effective Diversification Fig. 4.12

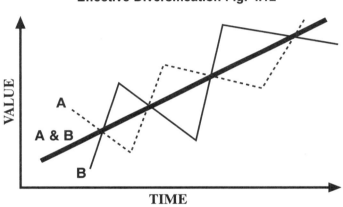

a given year. The years when the fund performance is down, the fund manager's goal is to minimize the downside by trading out of certain stocks and buying into others.

If we have only one asset class in our portfolio, there is nothing to offset the poor performance, to smooth out the natural volatility. As we have seen, periods of poor performance can dramatically impact the long term performance of your investment portfolio. (See Fig. 4.8 and Fig. 4.9 again.)

An asset class portfolio which is effectively diversified, minimizes the chances that one asset class will dramatically hurt the overall performance of your portfolio. This is a key concept. If the entire portfolio is invested in just one asset class, even though several funds have been used, the funds will all tend to move up and down together. There is no other way than effective diversification to soften a down market.

5
Efficient Frontier

In our discussions on standard deviation, we saw how each asset class has a probable rate of return based on historic performance. We saw how the high and low for each year is statistically predictable. We then reviewed the concept of regression to the mean. Regression to the mean refers to the long term tendency of funds, using a similar investment objective, to achieve an equivalent rate of return. Many funds advertise a specified objective but manage the money using a different criteria. This is called "style drift." So if the fund advertises an unusually high average return for its asset class, you may be accepting too much risk. It is reasonable to expect that the average growth rate during the succeeding five or 10 years may ultimately bring the overall return closer to the historic mean for this class. All of the historical data we have seen bears out this principle.

When selecting a mutual fund, there are three elements to carefully review: the objective of the fund, the historical standard deviation and the expense ratios. "Betting" on one particular fund based on performance alone is foolish and can be disappointing. You may be assuming too much risk, paying too much to achieve growth or buying the fund against the statistical probabilities of it maintaining its long term performance. Equivalent risks should be rewarded with equivalent returns.

Why does professional performance vary so much? I'm not certain anyone knows all of the historical reasons this happens. But we do know performance is random. A better question might be, "How did this fund achieve a higher than expected return?" Often the answer lies in the inordinate risk taken. There is no evidence to suggest a good year of performance predicts another good year will follow. In fact, the evidence suggests quite the opposite. We saw an example of this with Bogle's research in Chapter Three. A good performance in one year may be a precursor to a bad year coming up.

> *A good performance in one year may be a precursor to a bad year coming up.*

STYLE DRIFT

Random performance brings us to another important concept, style drift. With today's technology, information about various securities is known by the professionals very quickly. In fact, it is virtually impossible for any one professional manager to gain a significant edge over another. As a result, if a fund's performance stands out, a little investigation may disclose specific reasons for their "excellent" performance. The fund manager may have taken risks outside of the stated objectives of the fund. They may have "bet" heavily on one sector of the economy, like technology, while ignoring another sector, medical, for instance. Maybe they made a timing move which actually worked out. But most certainly, it is rarely based on a repeatable skill. A hunch is not a skill.

Fortune, in their February 17, 1997 article about investment performance asked this question of investors, "Why are there not more Peter Lynches?" Years after Lynch retired, the new manager of the same fund invested 30% of the assets into bonds, even though the stated objective of the fund was aggressive growth. He bet interest rates would drop more. When the interest rates rose instead, the fund lost significant money. The fund investors were forced to assume an investment risk they didn't even know they were taking.

Another example of these unknown risks is "derivatives." These very sophisticated investments which hedge interest rates are used to increase yield in the portfolio. In many cases, a fund will not specifically disclose any risks associated with this tactic or even mention they are using it.

EFFICIENT MARKETS

In March 1996, *Money* published an article detailing the historical performance of actively managed funds. Almost 85% of the active managers studied, failed to match the passive market index. A subsequent *Fortune* article showed that even in down markets, the broad based market often outperformed the active managers.

In years past, research and observation paid handsome dividends for both investors and money managers. But, computer technology has become the great equalizer. The efficiency of the markets support the impact instantaneous knowledge has had on investment results.

Again, the incredible pressure on fund managers to achieve superlative performance can cause fund managers to take inordinate risks or make decisions based

Randomness of Manager Performance (Fig. 5.1)

Year	Morningstar Manager of the Year and Fund	1987	1988	1989	1990	1991	1992	1993	1994
1994	**Bob Rodriguez** FPA Capital FPA New Income	5 2	58 51	38 42	70 20	16 17	15 5	51 51	[6] [3]
1993	**Jeff Vinik** Fidelity Magellan	—	—	—	—	—	—	[7]	50
1992	**Bill Dutton** Skyline Special Equities	—	9	47	42	59	[1]	19	48
1991	**Donald Yacktman** Selected American	67	14	69	53	[2]	73	Gone	—
1990	**Martin Whitman** Equity Strategies	77	6	73	[1]	93	71	45	Gone
1989	**Tom Marisco** Janus Twenty	98	31	[1]	18	2	85	84	84
1988	**Peter Lynch** Fidelity Magellan	61	[14]	18	Gone	—	—	—	—
1987	**Jerry Palmieri** Franklin Growth	[2]	76	65	11	76	81	65	14

Morningstar selects a "Manager of the Year" based on current year results and "the qualities of courage, discipline and independence that bring shareholders long term profits." However, judging from the inconsistent results achieved in the years following the manager's selection, the predictive value of the Manager of the Year is highly questionable. Figures shown above are percentile rankings (1 = top 1%, 100—bottom 1%) relative to other funds in the same mutual fund investment objective. Boxed rankings are rankings for the year in which the fund manager won the award.

on short term hunches to achieve short term results. As a "core" investor, you want to be making your investment decisions based on long term performance and asset class results, not short term risks designed to attract other investors.

Fund managers get paid on how well they perform in a given year. You need long term excellence. Your portfolio strategies should be driven by long term decisions made to protect your capital and enhance your returns, not on a portfolio manager's need to win or keep his job another year. In Fig. 5.1, you can see the historical longevity of some fund managers with some noted "name brand" funds. Long term growth depends upon consistency. Remember the key Alchemy factors— patience and persistence.

In summary, the efficient market theory says there are only two ways a manager can outperform other managers. They must either choose a diametrically opposite investment direction and then be right or outsmart all the other geniuses with superior stock selection. If they guess interest rates will rise and they do, the manager wins. If they are wrong, then they lose and so does the entire portfolio. If they believe "hi-tech" is going to soar, medical is going to decline and housing will rebound, they win. But a hunch is not a long term tactic you can count on for 30 years. What percentage of the time will they be right? How much are you willing to "bet" on their ability to be right? Core dollars are too precious to risk on a hunch. I am reminded of the movie *Other People's Money*. Danny DeVito was sitting in front of a computer screen scanning for "deals." He found an opportunity and then was able to corner the market and take over the company. While there are still opportunities for smart investors and money managers to take advantage of research and hunches, I'm not sure I would want to build my financial security on somebody's ability to do this year after year.

THE EFFICIENT FRONTIER

The power of the efficient market and the virtual impotence of the active managers to beat the market in recent years is well-documented. The concept of the efficient frontier is a different concept. The efficient market strategy says all market information is known instantaneously. There is little opportunity to gain an edge from the flow of information. In contrast, the Efficient Frontier is used to determine the optimum asset allocation mix for your invested capital. How much should you place in each asset class to achieve the highest probable portfolio return? Keep in mind you want to optimize yield and minimize risk.

For instance, let's suppose we are measuring international large cap with U.S. large cap. The international asset class has an average rate of return of 15.6% and a standard deviation of 21.2. (You may recall a standard deviation means most of the time. The returns will be ±21.2, a range between a plus 36.8% and -5.6%.)

The large cap, average rate of return from 1964–1994 is 15.9% and the standard deviation of risk is ±13.9. Again, this means most of the returns will vary between a plus 29.8% and -2%. Here is where it gets interesting. We saw that by combining the two asset classes, you can actually increase performance and decrease risk. The trick is to find the optimum allocation of capital for each asset class to produce the most efficient return. Efficient is defined as highest return for the lowest risk. Finding the optimum combination of investment mix is the purpose of the efficient frontier.

Using a computer analysis to track the historic data, we can create a curve like the one shown in Fig. 5.2. The edge of the curve closest to the Y axis is the optimum combination for just two asset classes. When we combine multiple classes, the

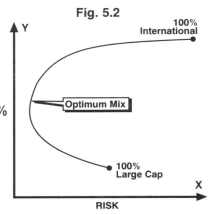

Fig. 5.2

curve changes, but the optimum allocation will remain the point nearest to the Y axis. The efficient frontier predicts the highest potential rate of return for the combined classes with the lowest potential volatility (measured by the standard deviation.) Any other combination of capital

Historic Returns by S&P 500 With EAFE (Fig. 5.3)

S&P 500 EAFE	Annualized Return	Total Return	Growth of a Dollar	Standard Deviation
100 0	12.29	1514.11	$16.14	17.01
90 10	12.43	1565.37	$16.55	16.57
80 20	12.55	1606.27	$17.06	16.37
70 30	12.63	1636.24	$17.38	16.42
60 40	12.68	1654.95	$17.55	16.71
50 50	12.70	1662.17	$17.62	17.25
40 60	12.69	1657.90	$17.58	17.99
30 70	12.65	1642.39	$17.42	18.92
20 80	12.57	1615.94	$17.16	20.02
10 90	12.47	1579.11	$16.79	21.25
0 100	12.34	1532.58	$16.33	22.60

mix, which would produce a predictably higher or lower return but with a higher probability of risk should be rejected.

In Fig. 5.3, we can see the power of combining two dissimilar asset classes (EAFE & S&P 500). Notice, the annualized return rose to a maximum value of 12.70 at 50/50 and then fell to a low of 12.34 at 100% EAFE. Note the risk increased as more foreign stock was added. Notice how high the risk was when the portfolio was 100% EAFE (22.60).

What was the goal? Wasn't it to improve your portfolio returns *and* decrease risk? Let's now advance our discussion to combine three asset classes (T-Bills, EAFE and U.S. Large Cap) to see how to accomplish our goal. We will build two hypothetical portfolios—portfolio (B) and portfolio (C). Look at Fig. 5.4. Point B this is based on the following percentages—T-Bills 30%, EAFE 30% and U.S. Large Cap 40%. The com-

Fig. 5.4

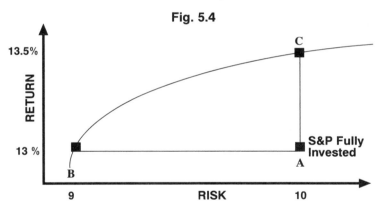

bined standard deviation of risk is 9. The combined return for this portfolio is 13%.

Now move over to point C (which is a higher risk, portfolio). Here, the allocation percentage is changed to T-Bills 20%, EAFE 40% and U.S. Large Cap 40%. The standard deviation increases to 10 and the return increases to 13.5%. Point A represents investing 100% of the portfolio into the S&P 500. Your return would have been 13% with a standard deviation of 10. To improve your return or reduce your risk, you would have two choices. You could either increase your return by moving from point A to point C. Or you could maintain the same return, but reduce your risk by moving from point A to point B. Either would be an improvement over staying fully invested in the S&P 500.

Remember, you are investing your "core" dollars. You want to preserve your capital, yet achieve a satisfactory return over a long time horizon. You want the highest return but the lowest risk. You also want to minimize the "ups" and "downs"of equity investing.

How is this accomplished? By combining several asset classes in an efficient manner using mutual funds. An efficient portfolio must not only use several asset classes, but also match these classes so they move efficiently together by determining and matching their coefficient correlation.

The efficient frontier curve is created for any number and combination of asset classes. By compiling this data and building an efficient curve, we are able to create an "ideal" portfolio for each client using the risk (volatility) assumptions each client is prepared to assume.

6
Selecting your Portfolio

By now, you have a feeling for the complexity of asset allocation. Not only do you have to identify the best asset classes, but you must combine them in an efficient method to maximize the return and minimize the risk. This is done by selecting classes with dissimilar price movements.

However, the most important piece is still undetermined. Which funds do you actually use to achieve these objectives? By now you have probably figured out I place relatively little value on active management of core assets. However, let me state clearly—prior to the information explosion sweeping the business world, portfolio managers were invaluable. Their ability to assess companies, determine value and time investment decisions was more of an art than a science. They brought great value to the investor. The active managers earned their fees. Today, I think much of the mystery of selecting quality stocks has been eliminated from most asset classes.

Is there still a place for an active manager? Certainly. However, the cost of accessing this expertise is much higher than market indices. You must ask, "Is the cost worth the anticipated reward?" Only the very wealthy, with large amounts of capital, can access the top managers at a low cost. The minimum investment is beyond the reach of most investors. What is the solution?

In this book, I have frequently referred to market based funds. They are primarily known as index funds. In the last chapter, I referred to recent articles showing that the historical results of index funds have generally outperformed the vast majority of active money managers in the broad market. I say active because active managers are continually trying to select the "hot" securities in order to achieve the highest return for their fund shareholders.

It is noteworthy when major financial publications, like *Money* and *Fortune*, write articles showing evidence that index funds have outperformed the active managers over an extended period of time. Even though these magazines create a lot of investor noise, they do identify trends of change. These magazines have denied the advantages of index funds for years.

DO INDEX FUNDS HAVE AN ADVANTAGE OVER ACTIVELY MANAGED FUNDS?

Remember, an index fund is a portfolio of secutities, which are purchased based upon a defined parameter. Index funds are called passively managed funds as contrasted to mutual funds, which are actively managed. Passive managers do not use any investment criteria to determine the best stocks whereas, the active managers of a mutual fund choose the best stocks based on a set of criteria determined by the fund managers and published in their investment policy statement.

It is important to remember that in the broad market of actively managed investments, active managers drive the value of stocks and the investors must accept the prices created by the supply and demand fluctuations in the market. In a totally passive fund, value is actually determined by the market forces. These market forces are the result of decisions these active managers make in much the same way the price a passive car buyer pays is determined by the active pricing decisions made by the manufacturers, the dealerships, the sales force and the buyers.

Contrary to what a lot of investors think, an index fund is not comprised of an equal investment in each of the stocks that make up the index. For instance, an S&P 500 Index Fund purchases shares of stock based on the "weighted value" of the largest 500 corporations. In 1998, the capitalized value of the bottom 450 stocks in this index, equals 50% of the entire value of the index. The top 50 stocks equal the remaining 50% of the value. A further analysis shows that 33% of the index is made up of only 24 stocks and only 4 stocks (General Electric, Microsoft, Coca-Cola and Exxon) equal 10% of the value of the index.

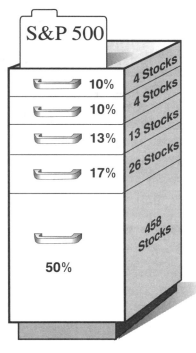

Active managers make buy and sell decisions to purchase the various stocks and the net asset value (NAV) of the fund reflects their investment decisions. If there were only two managers in the universe of managers, then those two would ultimately determine the direction of the market. The Index fund's NAV would then reflect the market value of those stocks.

What happens when active and passive managers decide to sell? Which portfolio will follow the prices back down? It is likely the passive fund will follow the active fund. Why? Active funds determine the market and passive funds follow the market. Over time, the impact should even out. However, investors need to understand there is nothing exceptionally safe about using Index funds over actively managed funds. The real advantage is that investors pay lower asset management fees for performance and they limit the impact of risks unrelated to market forces.

As I mentioned, there are many styles of indices. For instance, in the discussion on capitalization in Chapter 4, you may remember we divided the entire population of all publicly traded stocks into deciles. There are approximately 3,500 publicly traded stocks in the U.S. with capitalizations greater than $10,000,000. This means there would be 350 stocks in each decile. An investor could pick any decile as their target index. The 1 and 2 deciles would be the largest capitalized stocks. The 9 and 10 deciles would be the smallest capitalized stocks. You could purchase an index of just the largest and smallest stocks.

It is possible to also create an index of stocks for Europe, the United Kingdom, the Far East, and Asia. In fact, one of the most well-known indices is EAFE (Europe, Asia and the Far East). This way you are participating in the broad market. It is also possible to pick an index which selects only the value stocks for a given geographic area.

The point is, you are investing in an objective, market-driven process instead of purchasing professional management. Remember, you always pay for active management. Efficient market performance assumes the entire market will move up and down according to market forces and will be subject to less risk than if you invested in specific industries, technologies or products.

For instance, a broad index will include virtually all of the oil industry, energy stocks, high tech stocks, etc. If oil prices rise or fall, the result will be reflected in the overall performance of the index. But if the oil industry goes into the "tank," the index will also be insulated from the shock by the rest of the portfolio. The impact to your portfolio of a major economic trauma in one sector is much different than if you only own one sector. Your portfolio will be impacted proportionately, but not as severely as if you were invested only in the affected sector. Likewise, if oil prices rise and the industry has a huge increase in value, your portfolio will participate based only on the percentage you own. "Core" dollars are not meant to be invested in a "winner take all" portfolio.

This protection appeals to a lot of investors who want to protect their core dollars. They are interested in obtaining a smooth compound growth curve over a long time horizon. A speculator will be more concerned about stock movement in selected industries or sectors (i.e. medical, technology, etc.). A "core" investor will be more interested in participating in the 10 or 15 year performance of an entire economy.

If you are looking for the best strategy for your "core" capital, you need to decide whether or not you should place your hopes and fortune on active managers in specific sectors or the general market.

INSTITUTIONAL FUNDS VS. RETAIL FUNDS

There is an additional nuance to consider when selecting the proper fund group. Many funds are what

111

we call "retail" funds. This means the fund is marketed to the public through brokers, planners, discount houses, etc. More importantly, investors with as little as $100 can purchase fund shares.

Institutional funds are limited to investors with a much higher minimum investment of $250,000 or more to invest. What's the difference? First, retail funds are actively seeking small investors. They have higher advertising budgets and administrative expenses. Institutional funds seek pension plans and large investors. They have minimal marketing expenses.

> *Institutional funds are limited to investors with a much higher minimum investment of $250,000 or more to invest.*

There is another difference. Retail investors are often less sophisticated. They are more likely to pull out when the market drops precipitously or the market remains flat for a long period of time. They may have no one advising them or assisting them in their investment policy. Why is this important?

When a fund receives significant redemption requests, the fund must immediately liquidate holdings. They may be forced to sell large positions in certain stocks. Not only does this further compound the market reaction, but it also creates significant expenses. Who do you think pays these expenses? The net sellers have received their sale proceeds based on the current Net Asset Value (NAV) the day they sell. The remaining shareholders, the remaining investors, must now bear the burden of the selling expenses. Not only are they hammered by the possibility of dropping prices, but they are further impacted by the internal expenses incurred by the fund when the sellers "deplaned."

There is a further cost. Since the fund has had to liquidate their positions to match the redemptions, there may be additional income taxes due from the sale of unrecognized gains to the remaining shareholders. Deferred gains which had not been recognized may be sold to maintain a balanced portfolio and meet the liquidation requirements.

Contrast this to the institutional fund which has sophisticated investors. These investors do not run for shelter at the first sign of potential loss. A downturn in the market does not cause them to head for cover. They are long term investors and understand market fluctuations are just a part of the game.

In a conversation I had with one portfolio manager for a large pension fund, she estimated that it could take three to four years for investors in a popular retail fund to recover their losses if a sudden downturn caused a "run on the bank" by retail investors. Institutional funds can insulate you from many of these problems. This is just another reason to consider institutional funds for your "core" dollars.

ASSET MANAGEMENT FEES, EXPENSES AND 12(B)1 FEES

Why is it important to consider costs? Active money managers charge a significant asset management fee to manage the portfolio they have carefully crafted. Index funds, since they are passive funds, charge minimal fees.

Asset management fees are deducted from your account daily to reimburse the fund for the cost of selecting and reviewing the portfolio. These fees can range from a low of .10% to over 2.50%. The fund uses these fees to pay for the fund's overhead, professional staff, rent, telephone, etc. In addition, most funds also charge a .05%-.25% annual fee for expenses. These costs usually go for advertising and marketing. Another cost is the 12(b)1 fees. A 12(b)1 fee refers to the SEC regulations which allow funds to charge investors marketing fees. These fees range between .10% and .50% and compensate the marketing arm for "finding" the money.

It is rare to find either 12(b)1 fees or expense fees in an index fund. The asset management fee for an index fund normally ranges between .10% and .50%. International funds have higher fees plus a foreign tax which is applied to every fund.

TRADING COSTS AND TURNOVER

There is an another element, which is often overlooked— trading costs. These costs are not expressed in the prospectus because they are variable. But a fund which relies on active management to achieve returns, will, out of necessity, have higher trading costs than a passive fund which uses a buy and hold strategy. This trading causes turnover. You can determine the turnover effect by asking the fund directly or looking up the fund's turnover ratio in a resource like *Morningstar*. It is not unusual for an actively managed fund to have a turnover ratio in excess of 100%. This means a significant portion of the gains in a given year will be recognized as taxable income.

Clearly, the active manager must earn an additional return (often 2% or more higher), year in and year out, for their fund performance to equal the passive, index fund approach. Which one do you think you should choose? I will remind you that fewer than the 15% of the active managers have beaten the passive funds on a gross basis in recent years.

NOISE

The financial "pornograph-ic" magazines will suggest you follow their advice and pick the best performing funds. This is referred to as "chasing yield." By the time you read about it, it is probably too late! The newsletter people would suggest you follow their rec-ommendations. The financial planners pick their favorites. Everybody has a plan, an approach, a strategy. Everybody has an idea on who is the best or is going to be the best. But nobody really knows for sure.

> *I will remind you that less the 15% of the active managers can beat the passive funds on a gross basis.*

As a savvy investor, you must ultimately make a choice, unless you are going to stick your money under your mattress. This is why we believe using index funds for your "core" dollars is the best tactic. Index funds have the lowest expenses. They are less likely to be ambushed by a bad market. In addition, index funds have had one of the best track records in recent years. There is a system to the process. If you want to pursue money managers, do it with your speculative dollars.

HOW TAXES HURT PERFORMANCE

Let's look at the impact of taxes on fund perfor-mance if you are not invested in a tax exempt vehicle

(IRA, TSA Variable Annuity, etc.). Funds all report returns, net of expenses, but not net of taxes. If you select funds which have high trading costs and turnover, any analysis of the gains needs to include taxes.

Take an extended bull market which sees the S&P 500 grow by 100% during a three to five year period. In a passive fund, these gains will be "protected" because the stocks are not being traded. In an active fund, with a turnover of 100%, most of the gains will be recognized for tax. What impact does that have on a 100% return?

As an investor, you lack control over the timing or the amount of the tax. Using the Warren Buffet approach (just buy and hold), an institutional fund will typically shelters 85% of the taxable gain each year. Why? Because the institutional funds trade the stock in their portfolios less often. If the turnover ratio is only 15%, this means 85% of the gains will escape tax that year. A buy and hold fund strategy coupled with funds which have low turnover will shelter your gains from one year to the next. Say, for instance, you earned 10% on $100,000. That's $10,000 of gain. If all of it was exposed to taxes the earnings would be reduced to $7,000 (30% tax bracket). Instead of earning 10%, you netted only 7%.

Contrast this to a passive fund that only recognizes 15% of the gain. The tax on $1,500 in a 30% tax bracket would be $450. The net yield would be 9.6%.

The remaining gain continues to compound and might never be taxed if the funds are held until death. Otherwise, those gains are taxed when they are distributed.

CONTINGENT DEFERRED SALES CHARGES

By chasing returns, you will trigger your entire unrecognized gain for tax. You may also pay fees to make the transfer. Sometimes there are contingent deferred sales charges. Even if you select a different fund within the same family of funds, to avoid large external transfer fees, you still must pay tax on the gains.

Chasing yield only increases your chance of being wrong, moving in the wrong direction, or making the wrong selection of sector, industry, country, etc. But if you buy index funds and spread the risk among several countries and companies, you increase the probabilities of your portfolio eventually increasing in value and maintaining a smooth growth curve.

In summary, chasing return causes most investors to commit the four most critical investment errors.

1. Paying unnecessary taxes (turnover)

2. Incurring internal or external transfer fees

3. Losing the compounding effect of growth

4. Paying high asset management fees

You enhance your chance of attaining long term financial success when you:

1. Purchase market returns, instead of individual stocks or sectors.

2. Hold your position instead of trading to another approach frequently.

3. Select dissimilar indices to minimize volatility and maximize growth.

7
Foundation for Successful Investing

In the introduction, I outlined nine factors which we believe every investor should use to implement their investment program. If implemented correctly, a portfolio will be efficient and effective.

In the last chapter, I discussed in some detail, the most important problems and concerns every investor faces. Many investors try to solve their concerns by chasing yield. They shift from one fund to another hoping to ride the "wave" of high returns.

By avoiding the critical mistakes most investors make, you can achieve long term success in the market. Let's summarize these issues to make certain we completely cover them in a concise and usable format.

1. Paying no sales loads (Front and Back End)

2. Paying low cost advisory fees (less than 1.0% annually)

3. Paying low asset management fees (less than 50 basis points)

4. Incurring low trading costs

5. Paying low expense ratios

6. Protecting against excessive taxation of profits

7. Achieving a measurable performance benchmark

8. Attaining wide diversification of your assets

9. Having immediate access to your money

1. Eliminate sales loads (front and back end)

Some planners sell mutual funds with an initial 1%-5% front end load on your initial investment. Instead of investing $10,000, only $9,500 is actually deposited into your account. Many planners offer funds with no initial charge, but have a contingent deferred charge. If you want to liquidate before the stated period (usually six to seven years), you are penalized by the contractual amount. This back end load usually reduces from 6%-7% down to 0% as you "burn" off the charge. Having a surrender charge minimizes your flexibility. If you want to change investment vehicles you will have to pay a fee (the load). A true "no-load" has no charges for investing or for surrendering.

Ask yourself what services you are really receiving from your planner or advisor.

The controversy between buying "no-load" and "load" funds has persisted for many years. Philosophically, why should you have a significant reduction at the outset of your investment? Analysts argue the reduction is made up by having a lower asset management fee during the holding period. However, it can take several years for the difference to be recaptured. I personally favor "no-load."

2. Low cost for the advisory service

Fee planners charge advisory fees. Ask yourself what services you are really receiving from your planner or advisor. They should be helping you understand, on a regular basis, the performance of your program. This can be done through regular reports or with personal meetings. Your planner should be able to explain to you what has happened to your investment and perhaps why.

Most advisors will charge 1.5% to 2.0% annually for their services. I feel this is much too high except for very small accounts. These fees should be closer to 1% and then decline as your assets grow.

3. Low cost for investing the funds

Unless you purchase your funds wisely, you may be overpaying asset management fees for the funds you purchase. Remember, asset allocation can include actively managed funds. These fees have been rising despite the tremendous increase in assets under management. Unfortunately, studies show funds with higher asset management fees actually underperform funds with lower management fees. This just means you do not have to pay extra for performance.

Again, based on the last few years, the best way to achieve maximum performance has been to purchase index funds. Be careful, every fund family can point to at least one fund which has had exceptional performance. But which one? And when? Avoid buying a fund family because one fund has done exceptionally well. The key to compounding your money is to pick a superlative portfolio of funds and then ride it for 20 or 30 years. Chasing yield will cause an investor to:

- Pay unnecessary income taxes on the recognized gains

- Pay fees for making transfers
- Inhibit the chain of compound returns by incurring those additional expenses.

I suggest a buy and hold strategy. Buy the market and hold on for the duration.

4. Low trading costs

Again, most actively managed funds have high turnover. They sell their ability to judge the best stocks. This means they have to buy and sell many different stocks to achieve acceptable results. Every time they buy or sell, they incur trading costs which are never reported. If a fund has inordinately high trading costs, it could reduce the fund performance by .10% or more. In addition, turnover causes each investor to recognize taxes on capital gains. In many cases, the taxes caused by turnover could have been deferred. Avoid funds with high turnover ratios unless you buy it within a tax exempt vehicle like an IRA or 401(k) plan.

5. Low expense loads

In addition to asset management fees, most funds charge expense fees to cover administration and marketing costs. If you compound the savings from lower expense fees and lower management fees, you will find it amounts to a significant potential gain in your account.

6. Protection against excessive taxation of profits

I discussed this in point number four, but it bears mentioning again. If your turnover is high, then you receive virtually no tax shelter from holding on to your mutual funds. Not only do you lose by paying higher taxes but you also must pay higher trading costs. By contrast, an index fund shelters nearly 85% of the gains which are typically deferred until you liquidate your account. You have a unique tax shelter and if you never liquidate these gains, they may be permanently deferred at death because capital gains are not taxed at death.

7. A measurable benchmark for performance

How do you know if your portfolio is performing according to acceptable standards? Who sets those standards? I suggest using index benchmarks as a way of deciding how well your actively managed funds are performing. If you discover the funds you own are significantly under-performing the benchmarks, I suggest shifting to funds which consistently perform more in that asset class.

Remember there is a difference between an average return and an annualized return.

8. Wide diversification of your assets

In previous chapters, I have discussed the real value of diversifying efficiently. If your assets are not diversified by asset classes (which means a number of clearly defined markets), you are missing a real opportunity to take advantage of dissimilar price movement as a way to smooth out your compounding growth curve. If you are fully invested in the same basic asset classes, then your compounding portfolio return will be reduced as the market see-saws. Remember there is a difference between an average return and an annualized return. The average return is arithmetic—it is the sum of the returns divided by the number of years. The annualized return considers the timing of the returns. It weights each year's performance. The difference can be significant.

It is my recommendation that you consider using a variety of asset classes. It is important to use the asset class correlation coefficient to match the growth characteristics with your selected funds. Dissimilar price movement helps you smooth the return curve and potentially increases your investment results.

9. Immediate access to your money

If you hold your assets in the name of the brokerage company, you have to obtain permission from your broker or planner to access your own funds. The ideal accounts allow you to hold your funds in your name, so you can access them whenever you must. The advisor has a power of attorney to shift your funds, but never to liquidate your funds into their own account. You can have your money immediately upon request.

SUMMARY

All of these factors can work for you or against you. Most investors do not have time to research and understand the impact these elements have on their long range goals. They instead, delegate the responsibility to someone they trust. Unfortunately, it is difficult to find someone you should *truly* trust.

You must rely on referrals and references. Don't be afraid to ask to speak to clients who will attest to the service and integrity of your planner. Obviously, you will get only positive recommendations. But by thoroughly interviewing references, you can get a picture of what to expect.

Nobody is perfect. Every planner has weaknesses and a potential down side. But if the person is honest, has a long track record of dealing with the same clients and can demonstrate his own financial success, then you probably have a valuable planner.

8
How To Get Started

After reading all of this, are you excited about getting started and trying to implement some of this information to see if it works? It is important to know yourself and be consistent with your values. Unless you are absolutely truthful about your own propensity for risk, you will never be content.

Where do you start? How do you determine your portfolio structure? First, you need to determine your risk tolerance. How much risk can you really stand? Then define your investment objectives. What exactly are you trying to accomplish? And look at your time horizon. How long are you going to be accumulating? How long are you going to be spending? Answer these easy questions and see if the results of your answers match what you think your investment style should be.

Risk Tolerance

You just received a substantial sum of money. How would you invest it? (Mark the most appropriate answer.)

I would invest in something that offered moderate current income and was very safe.   *1*

I would invest in something that offered high

current income with a moderate amount of risk. **2**

I would invest in something that offered high total return (current income plus capital appreciation) with a moderately high amount of risk. **3**

I would invest in something that offered substantial capital appreciation even though it had a high amount of risk. **4**

Which of the following statements best describes your reaction if the value of your portfolio suddenly declined 15%? (Select one)

I would be very concerned because I cannot accept fluctuations in the value of my portfolio. **1**

If the amount of income I received was unaffected, it would not bother me. **2**

I would be concerned about even a temporary decline even though I knew this was a long-term growth investment. **3**

I would accept temporary fluctuations in my long-term investment that were due to market influences. **4**

Which of the following investments would you feel most comfortable owning? (Select one)

Certificates of deposit **1**

U.S. Government securities **2**

Stocks of older, established companies **3**

Stocks of newer, growing companies **4**

How optimistic are you about the long-term prospects for the economy? (Select one)

Pessimistic	*1*
Unsure	*2*
Somewhat optimistic	*3*
Very optimistic	*4*

Which of the following best describes your attitude about investments outside the U.S.? (Select one)

Pessimistic	*1*
Unsure	*2*
May be an attractive investment	*3*
Provides very attractive investment	*4*

Risk Tolerance Total _____

Investment Objective

What is your primary long term financial goal? (Select one)

Wealth preservation or emergency savings	*1*
Education funding	*2*
Retirement planning	*5*
Long-term wealth accumulation	*10*

Which of the following best describes your investment objectives?

Preserving principal and earning a moderate amount of current income	*1*

Generating a high amount of current income   **2**

Generating some current income and growing my assets   **3**

Growing my assets substantially   **4**

Five years from now, what do you expect your standard of living to be? (Select one)

The same as it is now   **1**

Somewhat better than it is now   **2**

Substantially better than it is now   **3**

Ten years from now, what do you expect your portfolio value to be? (Select one)

The same as or a little more than it is today   **1**

Moderately greater than it is today   **2**

Substantially greater than it is today   **3**

What is your current income requirement (interest plus dividends) from this portfolio? (Select one)

More than 4%   **1**

2% to 4%   **2**

0% to 2%   **3**

What do you want to do with the income generated by your portfolio? (Select one)

Receive all income   **1**

Receive some and reinvest some   **2**

Reinvest all income   **3**

How do you consider yourself as an investor? (Select one)

    Conservative   **1**

    Moderate   **2**

    Moderately Aggressive   **3**

    Aggressive   **4**

Investment Objectives Total   ____

Time Horizon

When will you begin to take income from this account? (Select one)

    0 – 5 Years   **1**

    5 – 10 Years   **2**

    10 – 15 Years   **5**

    15+ Years   **10**

Current Age (Select one)

    Over 56   **1**

    46 – 55   **2**

    36 – 45   **5**

    20 – 35   **10**

Time Horizon Total   ____

Total Score   ____

Now add up your total score and read the risk description that fits your score. If you don't agree, go back and reread the questions. See if any of the answers you made are really not reflective of your true concerns.

A. 1-20 If your score was within this "A" range, you are very conservative and the idea of loss makes you extremely uncomfortable. However, it is important to review the elements of risk. Go back and re-read Chapter 2 on measuring risk. You need to come to grips with the type of risk you face regardless of what investments you make.

Remember the real question is not whether you might lose capital as much as *how* you might lose it? Are you going to lose capital through eroding purchasing power or through the "potential" loss of capital because you made poor investment choices? If you are older, you have probably already experienced this problem. Older investors must measure total income against inflation. There is little room for error. One idea is to split your capital between a guaranteed income and an equity return. If you are younger, then the solution for you is a lot easier.

A conservative young investor usually needs to increase the amount of capital in their Bucket ONE investments to overcome the fear of risk. If you already have $50,000 in Bucket ONE, then double it. If you have $100,000 in it, then increase your Bucket ONE to $150,000. In other words, build a cushion of safety under you, so that you can tolerate the multiple gyrations that might occur in Bucket TWO. The key to withstanding fluctuations in the market is to *not* look. Whether your portfolio goes up or down month or even quarter to quarter is not relevant.

How To Get Started

Historically, the markets have increased in value. Unless you want to play the guessing game and try to pick the winners, you have only two choices—you can sit on the side lines and become a victim of inflationary price pressure or you can invest in the markets as a whole and ride the storms. You might want to reread the chapter on the value indexing (Chapter 7).

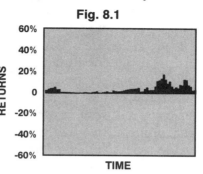

Fig. 8.1

Look at Fig. 8.1. Notice the returns are relatively low, but there are no downs. Does this feel good? If you are an "A", you'll look at this diagram and say, "I like it." If so, then you are definitely in the right place.

B. 20-40 A score in the "B" range indicates an openness to some volatility in your portfolio. Whether you are younger or older, the key to establishing an investment strategy is to target your objective carefully.

If you are seeking growth, ask yourself how much growth do you need? Refer to the WHATS, in Chapter 3 to determine the amount you'll need at retirement. Notice how Fig. 8.2 has very few lows. This can feel very comfortable as well. But unless you resolve the lows, you can't get the highs. Whether your goal is $1,000,000

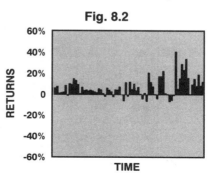

Fig. 8.2

during the next five years or $4,000,000 in 20 years, the problem is the same. How much do you have now and how much volatility can you tolerate? The less risk you can tolerate, the more you have to save or the more time you will have to take to achieve your target.

A "B" score means you have some tolerance for risk. You are comfortable accepting a minimum fluctuation in your portfolio. In this case, 60%-80% of your portfolio would be heavily weighted towards fixed investments with a two to five year maturity. The remaining 20%-40% would be invested in large cap value stocks, paying large dividends to increase your income.

This type of portfolio is well-suited to someone who has more than enough capital to meet their retirement objectives and to protect their capital from inflation. Income would be the primary objective for maintaining this portfolio. The investor would typically be focused on income and not care about growth.

C. 40-60 If your score totaled enough to fall into this category or above, you have a high tolerance for the potential ups and downs of the market. Your choice of portfolio should be determined by a WHATS analysis.

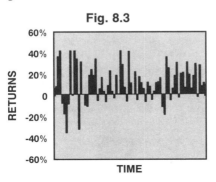

Fig. 8.3

Determine how much you need and how much you should save.

Simply, the more capital you need to build between now and your target retirement date, the more volatility you will have to absorb.

This diagram (Fig. 8.3) runs with the market. Look at those downs! If they get you in the gut, then back off from this portfolio. In 1973, the market took a big hit. In 1987, it did it again. This can happen.

20-40 If your score fell at this level, you should aim for 40% of your portfolio to be in the equity markets.

41-50 If your score is in this range, then you would probably want 60% of your portfolio to be placed in the equity markets.

51-60 An investor with this score would be at the upper end of the risk tolerance scale and would have 80% or more of their portfolio in the equity markets.

D. Above 61 This investor would probably have no fixed income investments in their portfolio. Is this a violation of the Bucket theory? Maybe. It would depend upon a closer look at total assets, planned expenses, life expectancy, and estate plans. This investor may have real estate, a solid business, or a family inheritance. There are numerous factors to consider before you select a 100% portfolio. Once you pick risk tolerance, you then need to pick your investment objective. Ask yourself, "how much income do I need to have at retirement?" Obviously, this number will be a key factor. Do the math and read the appendix on compound interest. This will give you a clear picture of how much capital you will need at retirement.

Epilog

Okay, we're done for now. We've made it through a complete analysis of what I feel are the most critical factors to consider when you plan your investment portfolio.

It is important to understand that there is no right answer for everyone. For some, market timing is the best answer. For others, stock selection will be the best strategy. For me, asset allocation with a buy and hold philosophy is the only way to really assure you will reach your long term objectives.

I can tell you this from my past experience, you will waiver on this approach. There will be times when the "noise" will be so loud, you will want to run for the hills. I know because I have had those same concerns. But truthfully, you need to look beyond the noise. You need to trust the market. It has always performed.

There is nothing different about today. There will always be wars and rumors of wars. There will be technological breakthroughs. Politics will ebb and flow. Tax brackets and laws will always change. The important thing to remember is that your time horizon is nearly 40 years (even longer for most of us), unless we are retired.

With a long time horizon, you have lots of room to be wrong. You only have to be right if your time horizon is less than five years. In that case, equities are probably not a good place to keep your money.

Review these principles again. Reread the book if necessary. Play around with the software. Read some of the good books on investing. You will discover there is a common thread among them all. There is no free lunch. There is no guaranteed method to achieve the best long term results. But there is a clear opportunity to participate in the growth of the markets by selecting a wise portfolio and then riding it over the peaks and valleys.

I sincerely hope this book will give you the confidence to try. Put your toe in the water. Try a while and see how it feels. Once you gain confidence, you will always put more into your account. But if you never start, then you will never see the results and feel the victory of long term success. Hopefully, this book will continue to contribute to your ultimate success.

God bless!

Guy@standel.com

Compound Interest Appendix

B oth Albert Einstein and Benjamin Franklin identified the power of compound interest. It is truly
the most amazing financial tool. However, if it is
not used wisely, it can defeat your financial objectives.

How? Debt is compound interest working in reverse.
What ever progress you make on your savings and invest
capital can be literally eroded or wiped out by interest on
debt. Many people have successfully used leverage (taking a loan and buying an asset and then selling it later for
a gain). However, for every one who has succeeded,
there are many hundreds who have failed.

In this section, I would like to help you earn a
Bachelor's degree, Master's degree and a Ph.D in compound interest. But before you can earn your doctorate,
you must start with your undergraduate degree. Nobody
likes to start at the bottom, but there is always a benefit.
It may only be a confirmation of what you already
know. But at worst, it will go quickly and assure you
that you know what you already know.

EARNING YOUR BA IN COMPOUND INTEREST

Suppose you have $1.00 and you can invest it at 6%.
What will it be worth at the end of the year? Answer:
$1.06. See how easy this is? At the end of two years you

**"Rule of 72"
Using 6% (Fig. A.1)**

Year	Amount
1	$1.06
2	$1.12
3	$1.19
4	$1.26
5	$1.34
6	$1.42
7	$1.50
8	$1.59
9	$1.69
10	$1.79
11	$1.90
12	$2.01
13	$2.13
14	$2.26
15	$2.40

would have $1.12 and the 3rd year you would have $1.19 and so on. The table (Fig. A.1) will show you the progression of growth over 15 years.

Now notice when $1 became $2. It happened in the 12th year. You can short cut this calculation by learning the rule of 72. Essentially, the rule of 72 says if you divide 72 by a specified interest rate, you will determine the number of years it takes money to double.

Likewise, if you divide 72 by the number of years you need for your money to double, it will tell you the interest rate you must earn to achieve your objective. Try it.

Suppose you want your money to double every six years. What interest rate must you earn? What about 10 years? What if you can only earn 9%, how many years will it take for you money to double?

Now check out the following chart (Fig. A.2) and see if you were accurate. If so, you have completed your undergraduate degree and are now ready for your MBA in compound interest.

See how it works? In order to make any progress with compound interest you must understand the rule of 72.

AN MBA IN COMPOUND INTEREST

I call the period of time it takes money to double an interval. If you want to reach your financial objectives by age 65, subtract your age and divide by the number of

Compound Interest Table (Fig. A.2)

Principal doubles with the rule of 72

Principal doubles the second time with the rule of 144

Principal doubles the third time with the rule of 216

Year	Rate								
	5.0%	6.0%	7.0%	8.0%	9.0%	10.0%	11.0%	12.0%	13.0%
1	1.05	1.06	1.07	1.08	1.09	1.10	1.11	1.12	1.13
2	1.10	1.12	1.14	1.17	1.19	1.21	1.23	1.25	1.28
3	1.16	1.19	1.23	1.26	1.30	1.33	1.37	1.40	1.44
4	1.22	1.26	1.31	1.36	1.41	1.46	1.52	1.57	1.63
5	1.28	1.34	1.40	1.47	1.54	1.61	1.69	1.76	1.84
6	1.34	1.42	1.50	1.59	1.68	1.77	1.87	1.97	2.08
7	1.41	1.50	1.61	1.71	1.83	1.95	2.08	2.21	2.35
8	1.48	1.59	1.72	1.85	1.99	2.14	2.30	2.48	2.66
9	1.55	1.69	1.84	2.00	2.17	2.36	2.56	2.77	3.00
10	1.63	1.79	1.97	2.16	2.37	2.59	2.84	3.11	3.39
11	1.71	1.90	2.10	2.33	2.58	2.85	3.15	3.48	3.84
12	1.80	2.01	2.25	2.52	2.81	3.14	3.50	3.90	4.33
13	1.89	2.13	2.41	2.72	3.07	3.45	3.88	4.36	4.90
14	1.98	2.26	2.58	2.94	3.34	3.80	4.31	4.89	5.53
15	2.08	2.40	2.76	3.17	3.64	4.18	4.78	5.47	6.25
16	2.18	2.54	2.95	3.43	3.97	4.59	5.31	6.13	7.07
17	2.29	2.69	3.16	3.70	4.33	5.05	5.90	6.87	7.99
18	2.41	2.85	3.38	4.00	4.72	5.56	6.54	7.69	9.02
19	2.53	3.03	3.62	4.32	5.14	6.12	7.26	8.61	10.20
20	2.65	3.21	3.87	4.66	5.60	6.73	8.06	9.65	11.52

years it takes money to double. Here's an example. Suppose you are 40 years old. If you are earning 6% on your capital, your money will double every 12 years. How many intervals do you have?

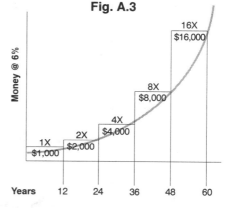

Fig. A.3

Answer: Subtract 40 from 65 = 25. Divide by 12 = 2.1 intervals. So if you have $100,000, you would have $400,000 by 64. Your money would be worth $200,000 by age 52 and $400,000 by age 64.

Let's assume you are able to earn 10%. Now your money would double every 7.2 years. How many intervals would you have? (25 divided by 7.2 = 3.5). This means your $100,000 would become $1,000,000 by age 65. Unfortunately, higher interest means higher risk and very few people are willing to accept higher risk, unless they understand the risk and what happens if they don't take it.

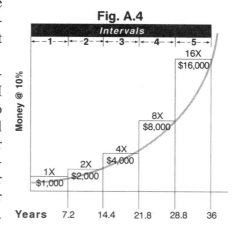

Fig. A.4

In the main section of the book, I covered the two risks everybody will face. They either risk losing their capital (volatility) or risk losing their purchasing power.

Most people agree that the inflation risk is guaranteed to happen. Loss of capital, historically, has a timing issue. You lose money only if you are forced to liquidate at the wrong time.

FRACTIONAL INTERVALS

We now know $1 doubles to $2 in a specified period of time. How long does it take $2 to become $3? Or $4 to become $5? Let's look at the problem and determine the answer. In Fig. A.5 it takes a full interval for $1 to become $2.

In the 2nd interval, $2 becomes $4. This means $2 reaches $3 at the half way point. If we use 6%, then $2 becomes $3 in the 6th year. However, at 10%, our $2 becomes $3 during the middle of the 3rd year.

Now, let's look at when $4 becomes $5.

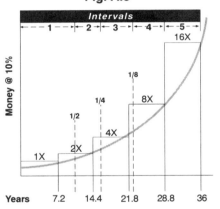

Fig. A.5

This occurs in the 3rd interval. The original $1 becomes $4 dollars at the beginning of the 3rd interval and then grows to $8 by the beginning of the 4th interval. Obviously, $4 becomes $5 sometime during the 2nd and 3rd year and so on.

Compound interest is not a linear relationship. It is geometric. A linear progression is 1, 2, 3, 4, etc. But a geometric progression 1, 2, 4, 8, 16, 32. See how much faster it grows. You can estimate the growth using the rule of 72. It is not perfect, but it will get you close. The point of this analysis is to show you how powerful

140

compound interest can really be. Think of it. What took nearly 12 years (using 6%) to accomplish in the beginning, took only approximately 6 years in the 2nd interval. And what took 6 years to complete, only took 3 years in the 3rd interval. Compound interest becomes more and more valuable the longer you stick with it.

That's why you never want to break "the chain of compound interest." What happens if you do? You go back to the beginning of the curve and start over. Most people fail to maintain the chain. They break for a variety of reasons. When they start again, they start at the beginning. It takes so long for the results to show. Let's face it, watching $1 grow to $1.06, then $1.13 is not

exciting. Watching $1 grow to $2 over a 12 year period is probably discouraging. Most anyone would become impatient. But there is a principle here you must understand.

Before I tell you the principle, let me ask you a question. There is an economic term for that first interval. Do you know what it is called? Everything has a an acronym or term derived by the creator. Give up? Well, I call it BORING. That's right, boring. Why? Because it takes so long. People become discouraged and quit. They quit just when the results are beginning to grow. Compound interest is a little like priming a pump. It takes a long time to see any results, but when it happens, the benefits are wonderful!

NOW FOR YOUR PH.D.

You've earned your Masters in compound interest. Now for your Ph.D. We've seen how compound interest works. We've discovered the power of the intervals and we've seen that we must never break the chain of compound interest. Before we start on our Ph.D however, let me give you the principle. You can *never* get to the next interval (2nd, 3rd or 4th intervals, etc.) until you have successfully completed the first one. Remember, if you break the chain of compound interest, you always go back to zero.

There are only two ways to accelerate the compound interest curve. You can either take more risk or you can invest more money. These are the only two factors you can affect. So if you are unhappy with how long it is taking you to accomplish your objective, you will need to decide which factor you should change. You can either invest more or risk more. Otherwise you are forced to stay status quo.

HOW MUCH DO I NEED?

We've seen how long it takes for compound interest to really start to pay off. Assume you are 45 years old and want $100,000 of retirement income.

This is not an easy question. Most people think of their retirement income in terms of today's dollars. But they don't factor into account loss of purchasing power caused by inflation. Look at Fig. A.6. Assuming you are at the retirement age of 65, if you want $100,000 of purchasing power (and can earn 6.25% every year), you will need $1,600,000. But if you expect to have your income keep pace with inflation, you will need $2,150,266 to keep up, if you retire at age 75. (This assumes 3% inflation.) If you retire at age 85, you will need $2,889,778 in

142

No Inflation Vs 3% Inflation (Fig. A.6)

No Inflation Capital Required (at 6.25%) if You Retire at Age . .

Desired Purchasing Power	Age 65	Age 75	Age 85
$50,000	$800,000	$800,000	$800,000
$100,000	$1,600,000	$1,600,000	$1,600,000
$150,000	$2,400,000	$2,400,000	$2,400,000
$200,000	$3,200,000	$3,200,000	$3,200,000

3% Inflation Capital Required (at 6.25%) if You Retire at Age . .

Desired Purchasing Power	Age 65	Age 75	Age 85
$50,000	$800,000	$1,075,133	$1,444,889
$100,000	$1,600,000	$2,150,266	$2,889,778
$150,000	$2,400,000	$3,225,399	$4,334,667
$200,000	$3,200,000	$4,300,532	$5,779,556

order to maintain your purchasing power.

But what if, you can earn 8%? Obviously, then you will do much better. Fig. A.7. shows that you only need

No Inflation Vs 3% Inflation (Fig. A.7)

No Inflation Capital Required (at 8.00%) if You Retire at Age . .

Desired Purchasing Power	Age 65	Age 75	Age 85
$50,000	$625,000	$625,000	$625,000
$100,000	$1,250,000	$1,250,000	$1,250,000
$150,000	$1,875,000	$1,875,000	$1,875,000
$ 200,000	$2,500,000	$2,500,000	$2,500,000

3% Inflation Capital Required (at 8.00%) if You Retire at Age . .

Desired Purchasing Power	Age 65	Age 75	Age 85
$50,000	$625,000	$839,948	$1,128,820
$100,000	$1,250,000	$1,679,895	$2,257,639
$150,000	$1,875,000	$2,519,843	$3,386,459
$200,000	$2,500,000	$3,359,791	$4,515,278

$1,250,000 to produce the same $100,000 of purchasing power. But by age 75, to maintain the same $100,000 of purchasing power you would need $1,679,895 and $2,257,639 if you retire by age 85.

There is only one problem with this logic. Remember, you are age 45 today and you want $100,000 in today's purchasing power. That requires $175,351 (Fig.A.8). You need to have enough capital at age 65 to produce $175,351. So, at 8%, you need don't need $1,250,000. You really need nearly $2,200,000 and if you retire at age 85, $3,900,000. Inflation proofing today's income really increases the cost.

$100,000 at 3% Inflation
Fig. A.8

Age	Income
45	100,000
50	112,551
55	130,477
60	151,259
65	175,351

But, there is another problem. If you don't have enough capital today, it means you must also grow your capital at the same time you are withdrawing your income. Your capital must earn more than the income you are withdrawing.

There is no way you can accomplish this without creating more capital or taking more risk. To sustain a level standard of living, you must either have enough capital when you start taking your income or you will have to earn a sufficiently higher return to compensate for the need to increase your purchasing power.

Look at Fig. A.9. In order to earn $100,000 at age 65 (in an inflation free world), you would only need $1,250,000 (at 8%). If you could earn 10%, then you would only need $1,000,000. But we know inflation is the nemesis. So we have to factor in growth to overcome inflation. Your capital must be much greater. Look at Fig. A.10. To have $175,351 of income

If you are 45, to earn $100,000 at age 65 (Fig. A.9)

You will need this much Capital at this interest rate				
8%	9%	10%	12%	15%
$1,250,000	1,111,111	1,000,000	833,333	666,667

If you have this much Capital now	You'll need to save this much annually for 20 years			
$50,000	22,223	16,241	11,587	4,872	-
$100,000	17,130	10,764	5,714	-	-
$150,000	12,037	5,286	-	-	-
$200,000	6,945	-	-	-	-
$250,000	1,852	-	-	-	-
$300,000	-	-	-	-	-
$350,000	-	-	-	-	-
$400,000	-	-	-	-	-
$450,000	-	-	-	-	-
$500,000	-	-	-	-	-

($100,000 of purchasing power earning 8%) to keep pace with inflation, you will need $4,077,547. Why so much?

For your capital to grow at the same time you are withdrawing an income, you needed $1,250,000 at 8%. But to keep pace with inflation, it really requires you earn enough to grow your capital while taking the income. This is much harder to do. If you are conservative, you will find the extra risk quite uncomfortable.

The $4,077,547 provides enough capital to pay $175,351 annually and grow your capital so you will always be able to sustain a level purchasing power. So, how much more do you have to invest?

If we go back to Fig. A.9, the bottom of the chart shows how much you have to save if you are already investing. Assume you already have $50,000 working for you. Then at 8% you need to invest $22,223 annually until age 65. If you do that and earn 8%, you will have

Compound Interest Appendix

**For $100,000 Annual Purchasing Power, Payable in 20 Years
Adjusting for Inflation at 3%, You Actually Will Need an
Income of $203,279 (Fig. A.10)**

At this interest rate, You will need this much Capital				
8%	9%	10%	12%	15%
$4,077,547	3,624,486	3,262,038	2,718,365	2,174,692

If you have this much Capital now	You'll need to save this much annually for 20 years				
$50,000	84,011	65,369	51,081	31,034	13,240
$100,000	78,918	59,891	45,208	24,340	5,252
$150,000	73,826	54,414	39,335	17,646	-
$200,000	68,733	48,937	33,462	10,952	-
$250,000	63,640	43,459	27,589	4,258	-
$300,000	58,548	37,982	21,716	-	-
$350,000	53,455	32,505	15,843	-	-
$400,000	48,363	27,027	9,970	-	-
$450,000	43,270	21,550	4,097	-	-
$500,000	38,177	16,073	-	-	-

$1,250,000.

Here comes inflation again, Fig. A.10. You now have to invest $84,011 annually to get to your goal. If we look at 10%, the the annual amount you must save will reduce to $51,081. If you already have some capital working for you, then your job is easier. Look at $200,000 (Fig. A.10). At 8% you have to invest $68,733 each year, but at 10% you can accomplish the same job by investing $33,462.

This just proves the principle of more time—more money. The more time you have, the more your money will grow. The less time you have, the more risk you must take to reach your goal. There is no easy answer.

SUMMARY

Well, congratulations! You have just earned your Ph.D in compound interest. Mastering compound interest allows you to understand the importance of investing your money properly. By employing the principles in this book and holding your investments for an extended period of time, you can achieve economic freedom. Only those who want to get rich quick or try to beat the compound interest system risk failure.

Judging by the statistics, 92% of the population has taken the wrong path on this journey. You can avoid those same pitfalls by staying the course and properly using the investment principles outlined in this book. Go back now and review the simple steps every long term investor needs to follow to grow their capital. Go to page 117 for a review.

Glossary

Active Management
Professional investment specialist hired to select stocks whose expected performance will be greater than the market index averages. There are two different approaches: security selection and market timing. *Security selection* trys to find and purchase equities that will increase in value and sell those who have attained their optimum value. Inherent in this process is the belief the market has not accurately valued the stocks or that the manager can make this determination before anyone else finds out. *Market timing* is the manager's attempt to predict future market direction and anticipate the change before the market corrects. Multiple studies have shown there is no fail safe method to accomplish either objective.[1] Using market indices as the benchmark, there is no empirical evidence which can demonstrate consistent and predictable results from either method. When you factor in the cost of active management, numerous studies have shown over 80% of the active managers under perform the market.

Asset Allocation
The diversification of securities among distinct and separate categories of assets, such as cash equivalents, stocks, fixed-income investments, and natural resources (precious metals, real estate, oil and gas). Asset Allocation also refers to various

---

[1] SEI Research reports, June 1990, Vol. 6, No.3

sub-categories of securities like municipal and corporate bonds, various government securities as well as equity groupings by industry and market segment. Studies demonstrate that

Moderate Portfolio Mix

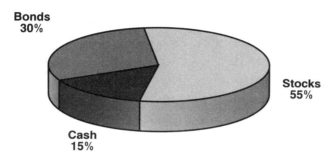

Bonds 30%

Stocks 55%

Cash 15%

the allocation of funds in various classes will impact the long term return and volatility of the investment portfolio. When making personal investment decisions, it is important to clearly define the expected rate of return desired compared to the amount of volatility you are prepared to experience. To optimize the value of an asset allocation program, it is important to choose an allocation of asset classes which will move in opposite directions to minimize volatility and optimize the compounded growth of the portfolio. Effective diversification matches the best asset classes with the optimum volatility factor you can sustain and still feel comfortable.

Correlation Coefficient
The probability of the market value of two or more securities moving in the same direction at the same time. If Security A increases in value, then what is Security B likely to do? If B increases in value, then the two securities are said to be positively correlated. However, if Security B declines in value, then the two securities are negatively correlated. If there is no pattern, (B moves both up and down with no relation to A),

Negative Correlation

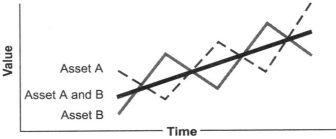

then they have no correlation. Correlation values range from +1 to -1. A +1 factor means the return for these securities will move in lockstep with each other, although not necessarily to the same degree. A -1 factor means the securities are likely to move in opposite directions. Why is negative correlation good? Dissimilar price movement occurs when we combine asset classes with low correlation or negative correlation. When this occurs, volatility should decrease, which will ultimately enhance the rate of return of the portfolio. Historic studies have demonstrated that by using low and/or negatively correlated portfolios, the annualized return is higher than if the portfolios attained the same return but were positively correlated. This is what we call effective diversification.

Dissimilar Price Movements
The predictable movement of different asset classes. When asset classes move in opposite directions, they are said to be negatively correlated (see Correlation Coefficient). By deliberately creating dissimilar asset class correlation in the portfolio, the natural volatility of all asset classes are offsetting each other to some degree. By smoothing out any wide fluctuations, the ultimate value of the portfolio should be appreciably higher than if all of the asset classes moved together over the same period of time. Studies have shown that when asset classes move dissimilarly, they become a valuable tool for reducing the volatility.

Diversification

A prudent method for managing investment risk. There are many different types of risk, such as interest rate risks, integrity risks, competency risks, in addition to market risks and economic risks. These unsystematic risks can be reduced by using different asset classes. Interestingly, diversification alone may not be effective if all of the assets are invested in similar asset classes. Many investors choose a wide range of mutual funds, thinking they have spread their risk. While they have diversified among funds, have they, in fact, diversified among style, market segment, national and international markets, etc.? What happens if the entire portfolio declines at the same time? If you owned a Stock Index fund which mirrors the S&P 500 and stocks in the Dow Jones, both would tend to move in the same direction at the same time. We call this ineffective diversification.

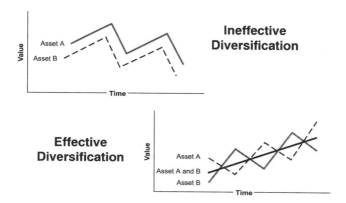

Effective Diversification

An asset allocation that is effectively diversified minimizes extreme price fluctuations by using a negative correlation coefficient. Intuitively, we know that diversification is good. It's just that certain types of diversification are better. Modern Portfolio theory is based on this premise. Markowitz, Sharpe and Miller showed in their 1990 Noble Prize winning thesis that securities which do not move together, optimize return and effectively cause most risk to be effectively diversified away. The optimum portfolio is still going to suffer some volatility. However, if you can minimize the extreme price fluctuations, it will smooth out the ultimate return. Comparing two portfolios over time, if they had the same average return, the one with the lowest volatility would have the highest total return.

Efficient Frontier

The optimization of probable risk (see: Standard Deviation), expected returns and correlation coefficients (dissimilar price movements). A spectrum of portfolio combinations is created in which the portfolios are measured on a graph line called the "efficient frontier." The line represents the expected return for a variety of asset mixes within the portfolio at each level of risk. The chart below demonstrates three different portfolios compared to a portfolio fully invested in treasury bills or U.S. Large Stocks.

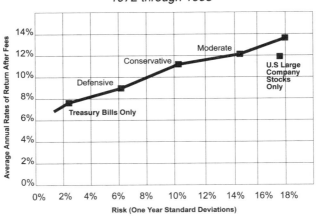

Efficient Frontier
A simulated comparison–balancing risk and reward
1972 through 1993

In this example, the moderate portfolio has the same ROR (12%) as the U.S. Large Company Stock fund. However, the historic risk (as measured on the Risk axis) is less (14.25 instead of 17.5). The ultimate result is the same net return but with less risk than if you were 100% exposed to the market in just the U.S. Large Company Stocks. Note too, that because the efficient frontier represents the mathematically and historically optimum return for any level of risk, it is impossible for there to be any portfolio above the line. The efficient frontier, then this is an effective tool to assist the investor in making the best choice based on the volatility he is willing to endure.

Efficient Market

A hypothesis which says the current market value reflects all the knowledge and value anticipated by a rational investor. In other words, with the speed of communication, and the advent of stock analysts pondering virtually every company movement, it is practically impossible for information to exist that is not already known by the market and previously factored into stock value by analysts. Spending time trying to uncover stocks whose value is yet to be realized has limited payback and is often futile. The theory goes on to say, the market price will always reflect the current value based on the entire body of information known at that time, making it virtually impossible to "beat" the market. Granted, the prices may not accurately reflect the true value of the stock at any given point in time, but it is unbiased, i.e., the tendency will not favor overpricing or underpricing.

Many models have demonstrated that throwing darts at the newspaper's stock listings have an equally good chance as any professional analyst to create a portfolio which will consistently outperform the market. Several academic scholars have demonstrated the randomness of price movements and suggest the only way to invest in the market is through effective diversification in multiple asset classes. (see Efficient Frontier).

Glossary

Efficient Portfolio

A portfolio which provides an expected return based on a measured level of historic risk. The result is determined by mathematically combining expected return, historic volatility and correlation coefficients to determine similar and dissimilar price movements. There is a most efficient portfolio for every level of risk. (see Efficient Frontier).

Expected Return

Yields in each asset class that are based on historic performance measured over an extended period of time (normally at least 20 years). Assuming there is no style drift and the economic elements remain static, the historic return should be a predictor of future return. Although these are purely theoretical returns, they provide a rational for calculations. They are in no way indicative of future performance. Historic economic tendencies change as government tax laws and judicial enactment impact investors and consumers. The prudent investor is attempting to maximize his return at a stated level of risk. The success of any strategy depends upon the assumptions. More important, the model must be adjusted to reflect sociological and economic changes.

Index Fund

A mutual fund which purchases equities in the same proportion as a recognizable standard (such as Standard & Poor's 500 Index). The objective is to have the fund mirror the performance of the specified benchmark.

Many institutional and non-institutional investors believe in the efficient market theory. As a result, they rely on the Index Fund performance to reflect the actual value of the market as a whole over an extended time horizon. Numerous magazine articles have documented the superlative performance of passively managed funds compared to actively managed funds.

Institutional Asset Classes

Funds representing specific asset classes to be used by large pension plans or large trust companies. Inherent in their design are low management costs, stable value and minimal outflows of redemptions. These are referred to as institutional asset class funds.

Generally, no-load institutional asset class funds have three defining characteristics: because the minimum investment is so high ($250,000 and up), typically, only sophisticated investors will be using the funds. This minimizes the potential outflow of capital in a down market because these investors know markets fluctuate. Second, because this capital is relatively stable, the inherent costs of investment management are much lower than for similar retail funds with $2,000 minimums. Administration costs are lower and asset management fees are less. These lower costs mean higher net returns to the investor. Third, because the class investment styles are stable and predictable, it further enhances the possibilities of distinguishing reliable long-term correlation between classes to identify similar and dissimilar price movements.

Redemptions occur at *Net Asset Value* (NAV). When a retail investor redeems their shares, the remaining shareholders must pay the trading costs of that redemption. Trades in an institutional fund are minimized because they are typically looking for long-term results. Some stock turnover occurs simply because a portfolio is dynamic. But generally speaking, institutional funds have significantly less turnover (85% less) and trading expenses than retail funds.

Empirical evidence shows passive index funds have historically outperformed actively managed funds. Many investors have discovered that asset classes offer a new way to diversify and reduce investment costs and capital gains taxes. By mixing institutional asset classes with dissimilar price movement, risk is reduced and returns may increase.

There is a study by Brinson Partners which attempted to

Determinants of Portfolio Performance

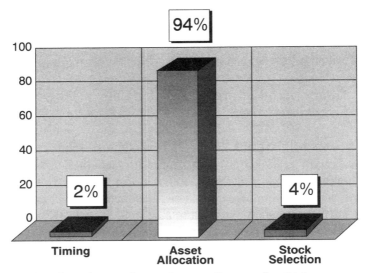

identify the primary determinates of return for 91 large pension plans over two different 10 year periods. The study showed that fund performance was impacted more by the asset class selections (more than 94% of the time) than by any of the other commonly used investment tactics. Stock selection and timing remain important determinants, however, asset allocation emerged as the dominant element to explain return.

Investment Policy Statement

A statement written to define your financial objectives, how much you can invest, what methodology you have selected and which tactics will be used to obtain an expected outcome. The investment policy statement should be customized to match your objectives and tolerance for volatility. Each investor should carefully evaluate their tolerance for portfolio volatility. The sleep factor is more important than any single investment decision you can make.

Optimal Portfolio

The portfolio best suited to your risk tolerance, determined after you have identified each efficient portfolio.

Once an investor understands the relative impact of dissimilar price movements on portfolio volatility, there is a tendency to accept more risk than originally intended, in order to achieve a higher ROR. By carefully measuring the relative risk you are willing to take for a commensurate return, the range of returns can be graphed on a risk curve or indifference curve. Practically speaking, few investors could actually develop such a curve. It would be difficult to actually quantify acceptable levels of risk relative to return. There are too many factors which come into play, (fear, reaction to the market, investment noise). But in a strategic sense, the *optimal asset mix* is the point along the *efficient frontier* which touches your *risk curve*. Hence, the *optimal portfolio* is the portfolio which has the highest expected return for the risk level the investor is willing to endure.

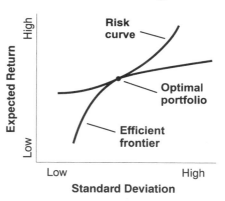

Passive Management

A strict buy and hold theory. It depends on market growth rather than stock selection or market timing. By selecting mutual funds which are based on market performance and holding them during a long time horizon, the investor is less likely to be negatively impacted by bad stock selection or mistakes in market timing.

Passive management should not be confused with no management. Selecting the right mix of assets, determining the appropriate allocation to achieve optimal dissimilarity, rebalancing the portfolio periodically to maintain real long-term optimization, requires considerable work. Through computer analysis of historical data, securities that will provide the most effective diversification and highest yield for a given level of risk must be identified and placed in the appropriate portfolio. One goal of passive management is to maintain the investor's position on the efficient frontier.

Portfolio Theory

Statistically measured theory that permits an investor to classify, estimate, and control both the kind and amount of expected risk and return. It is also called *Modern Portfolio Theory* or *Portfolio Management Theory*. MPT departs from traditional security analysis by shifting emphasis from analyzing market timing and selecting stock value to determine the price movement relationships between the individual securities which comprise the overall portfolio. As early as 1952, Harry Markowitz published an article with his colleagues in the *Journal of Finance,* which described how to combine assets into efficiently diversified portfolios. In 1990, along with his colleagues, he was awarded the Nobel Prize in Economics for this theory. They demonstrated that failure to account correctly for the dissimilar price movement among security returns was a major oversight. He demonstrated empirically that holding securities which move in concert with each other does not lower one's risk. Proper diversification can occur *only* when the portfolio of assets move in dissimilar directions at similar times.

Re-balancing

An adjustment which brings the portfolio back to the optimum point on the efficient frontier. It is expected that certain asset classes will outperform others over time. By rebalancing, you effectively buy low and sell high. You sell the top performing assets to purchase the worst performing assets under the theory. The lower performing assets are expected to rebound in the future. This is particularly dependent upon a strict adherence to asset class definition and the dissimilar price relationships of the classes.

Re-optimization

Another adjustment tool, which brings the mix of asset classes for the portfolio back to the efficient frontier. Factors may change from time to time which make the asset class combination less efficient than originally defined. Proper re-optimization should take into consideration any transaction costs associated with re-optimizing.

Risk

The possibility of financial loss and/or uncertainty of future gain. In a cyclical market place, the best measure of risk is volatility in the market. The less certain you become about the eventual outcome, the more risk you are assuming.

Historical investment variance or volatility (risk) uses standard deviation as the measuring tool (see Standard Deviation). The probability of a lower return should be reflective of a lower risk.There are only two basic risks: loss of principal and loss of purchasing power. You lose principal only if the underlying value of your investment is lower than your investment when you want to sell. The reason the value fell is immaterial.

Nondiversifiable risk (systemic risk) impacts all aspects of the world economy, as well as the financial markets and cannot be eliminated through diversification. *Diversifiable risks (nonsystemic)* can be minimized or eliminated through proper asset allocation. As a general rule, the market will not provide a significant return for a diversifiable risk.

The risk of losing purchasing power occurs through a loss

of value in the amount of goods and services the income from principal can purchase. Inherent in this risk is the need to systematically liquidate principal to purchase the same amount of goods and services. The primary cause of this risk is taxes and inflation.

Risk Tolerance

The amount of risk each investor is willing to take. Your tolerancecan change as you get older, achieve your objectives or change your financial circumstances. The investor is forced to choose between an expected rate of return on his principal and the risk exposure he is willing to take to receive an expected rate of return. Generally speaking, younger investors have the greatest tolerance for risk. A major problem occurs when the investor must take more risk to reach his retirement objectives.

Standard Deviation

A statistical measurement of a large number of events and how they vary from the average. For instance, say the average was 15, and the sample event was 10. The variance would be -5. In a totally random sample, with enough data, a graph of the variance of all events would ideally form a bell shaped curve. Because standard of deviation measures the variance from the average, it can tell an investor what the statistical chances are of losing money.

One full standard deviation from the average considers 68% of all events; two standard deviations cover approximately 95% of all events. For example, the following chart shows the probability of an investor earning an average return. The average annual expected return for the S&P 500 is 12.2%. We can expect that returns would fall between -8.4 and 32.8 (12.2 ± 20.6) approximately two-thirds (68%) of the time. The higher the standard deviation, the higher the risk.

Standard Deviation as a Measure of Risk
S&P 500 Index: Average annual expected return = 12.2%
Standard deviation = 20.6%

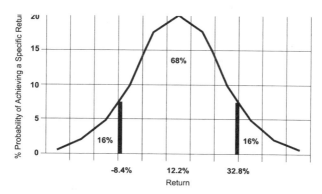

If two portfolios have the same expected return, the portfolio with the lowest variances from the average will create the greater compounding result.

Style Drift
The non-conformance of certain portfolio equities to the stated objective. Some portfolio managers, in an effort to create higher results, will select certain equities which are not within the acceptable range of risk or approved definition of capitalization, industry, equity selection, etc. The style of the fund "drifts" away from the fund objective and causes the investor to accept a higher level of risk than disclosed in the prospectus.

Variance
The amount the event deviates from the average. The Modern Portfolio Theory demonstrated that if you can reduce a portfolio's variance, it will actually increase the compounded rate of return. For example, assume Portfolio A ($100) is up 20% in one period but earned 10% in the second period. The Portfolio is worth $120 and averaged 10% each year. Portfolio B earned 10% in both years and is worth $121 at the end of two periods.

161

Two Portfolios With the Same Average Rate of Return

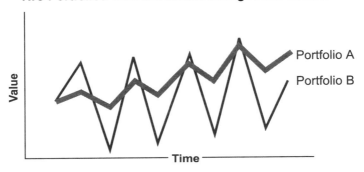

Portfolio A had a wider variance from the average.

If two portfolios have the same expected return, the one with the lower volatility will have the greater compounded value, hence the higher rate of return. Interestingly, the concept of variance is indifferent to market direction. Portfolio (A) with no dissimilar price movements, will move in accordance to the market cycles. As a result, it is unlikely to have a level rate of return. A passive portfolio (B), utilizing dissimilar price movement to minimize variance will likely outperform (A) even though (A) might have higher highs than (B). The concept of variance reduction should result in underperformance during certain periods of high returns. Ultimately, however, it assures a higher compounded rate of return. Computer simulations for the period 1972 to 1989, using reduced variance techniques on the cap-weighted S&P 500 and the DJIA indexes, produced a differential of about 350 basis points on the ROR. There does not appear to be another way to achieve variance reduction other than through dissimilar price movements.

Wrap (Fee) Account
A stated fee based on a percentage of assets is applied to a total portfolio. This fee covers all charges, including advisor costs, commission charges and reporting costs. It includes

selecting active money managers, custodianship, account reporting, tracking of manager's performance, transactions fees and consulting.

Wrap fees have been used by large brokerage firms to attract larger accounts. We see several disadvantages to Wrap Accounts. There can be many levels of fees. The published fee is generally 2.5% to 3%. There are also hidden costs such as trading commissions. These can impact the portfolio's future return. It is common for the fund managers to direct all of the trades through the referring brokerage firm. What is the guarantee the trading costs are the most competitive? Are they disclosed? Who is measuring the coefficient correlations and managing the reoptimization and rebalancing? It is entirely possible these fees could amount to 4-5% of your total assets annually and you would have no way of knowing. There is significant evidence the wrap fee will not produce superlative returns. Successful money managers today are not necessarily going to be successful tomorrow. What are you buying? We fail to see how wrap fees achieve effective diversification.